THE PATH

BY

MARTIN J. MCNAMARA

ISBN:1468017284
ISBN-13: 978-1468017281

DEDICATION

REGINA THUROW MY SOULMATE IN THIS
JOURNEY

CHAPTERS

i

1   Introduction   Page #8

2   Disobedience   Page #21

3   Love   Page # 81

4   Faith   Page # 124

5. Obedience   Page # 146

6. 12 Step Path   Page # 178

The Path

In Memory

Catherine and William McNamara

ACKNOWLEDGMENTS

PAT SUTAY

FOR ENCOURAGIN ME TO WRITE THIS JOURNEY

AUTHOR'S COMMENT

THE PATH IS MY PERSONAL JOURNEY
THROUGH THE BIBLE AND HOW IT CHANGED
MY LIFE.. I AM NOT A BIBLE SCHOLAR AND
APOLOGIZE IN ADVANCE FOR ANY BIBLE
INACCURACIES.

INTRODUCTION

OBEYING WHILE I WAS GROWING UP WAS DIFFICULT FOR ME. I GREW UP QUESTIONING EVERYONE. THE ROOT OF THIS LIES IN NOT TRUSTING ANYONE. I WOULD ALWAYS DOUBT WHAT PEOPLE WERE SAYING TO ME. GROWING UP WAS DIFFICULT AND I QUESTION TODAY WHETHER I TRUSTED GOD. FOR SOME REASON, I ALWAYS REBELLED IN SCHOOL AND DISOBEYED MY TEACHERS. I ALSO DISOBEYED MY PARENTS.

THE UNDERLINING THEME IN THIS BOOK IS ABOUT TRUST, LOVE AND FAITH AND WHY I FOUND IT DIFFICULT TO OBEY, TRUST AND

LOVE HUMANS AND GOD WHILE GROWING UP.

AS FAR BACK AS I CAN REMEMBER I FELT ALIENATED FROM MY PARENTS. I FELT VERBALLY ABUSED BY THEM. SO NATURALLY, I REBELLED AND AS A CATHOLIC FELT THREATENED BY THE NUNS AND PRIESTS. I WAS TAUGHT THAT GOD WAS A PUNISHING DEITY AND I LEARNED TO FEAR GOD. I FOUND IT IMPOSSIBLE TO OBEY SOMETHING I FEARED.

MY ADOLESCENT YEARS WERE FILLED WITH ANGER AND

RESENTMENT. I DISOBEYED TEACHERS, PRIESTS, AND MY PARENTS. I HAD VERY FEW FRIENDS. I BECAME ISOLATED AND REBELLIOUS.

I LEFT THE CATHOLIC CHURCH AND STARTED DRINKING DURING MY TEENAGE YEARS. I LEFT THE CHURCH EMOTIONALLY AND SPIRITUALLY YEARS BEFORE I PHYSICALLY WALKED OUT OF ITS DOORS. IN REALITY, BY SEPARATING MYSELF FROM THE CHURCH, I BECAME LOST SPIRITUALLY.

I FELT BETRAYED BY GOD. I FELT HE WAS PUNISHING ME FOR

MY DRINKING. I DRANK MORE IN DISOBEDIENCE TO GET EVEN WITH GOD. I FELT GOD HATED ME AND YET GOD SAVED ME TIME AFTER TIME WHEN I MESSED UP.

I FELT BETRAYED BY GOD. WHEN I WAS GOING THROUGH MY DIVORCE. BY NOT BELIEVING HE WAS THERE. I BECAME DISILLUSIONED BY NOT ACKNOWLEDGING HIS PRESENCE. THROUGHOUT MY DIVORCE., MY EX-WIFE WANTED TO REMAIN FRIENDS AND TODAY KEPT HER WORD. IN OUR MARRIAGE VOWS, WE NEVER PROMISED OBEDIENCE, BUT LOVE FOR ONE ANOTHER.

IN WORK SITUATIONS, I FOUND THAT OBEDIENCE WAS NECESSARY, BUT I STILL QUESTIONED THEIR AUTHORITY. MANY OF THE PEOPLE I WORKED FOR KNEW THE RIGHT PEOPLE, BUT THEIR WORK WAS POOR.

WHEN I JOINED ALCOHOLICS ANONYMOUS IN THE MID-SEVENTIES, I FOUND A SPONSOR. I WANTED TO TRUST HIM, BUT FELT HE WANTED TO RUN MY LIFE. I ALLOWED HIM TO RUN MY LIFE FOR SEVERAL YEARS. HIS DICTATORIAL STYLE DAMAGED ME TO THE POINT WHERE I TRUSTED NO ONE.

I NEEDED TO LEARN TO TRUST AND LOVE GOD THROUGH THIS FEELING. BY LEARNING TO BELIEVE IN GOD, HE ALLOWS THE RIGHT PEOPLE TO COME INTO MY LIFE AT THE RIGHT TIME, FOR THE RIGHT REASON.

I KNOW WHEN SOMETHING IS RIGHT – I FEEL IT IN MY HEART AND SPIRIT.

THE SPIRIT THAT IS RIGHT FOR ME IS BEING A CATHOLIC. A FORMER COUNSELOR REAWAKENED ME TO THIS PATH. HE TOLD ME TO LOOK TO GOD FOR EVERYTHING FOR LOVING AND TRUSTING GOD TO HAVING

SPIRITUAL PASSION FOR THE LIFE
OF OTHERS. IT'S CALLED
UNCONDITIONAL LOVE. I NEED
TO BE A BEACON OF
UNCONDITIONAL LOVE.

BY FALLING TO WORLDLY
TEMPTATIONS, I WAS BEING
DISTANT FROM GOD. FROM EARLY
ON IN MY CHILDHOOD, I LEARNED
TO AVOID ANY PUNISHMENT FROM
MY PARENTS. FOR SOME REASON, I
WAS A DISOBEDIENT, ANGRY CHILD
AND EXPLODED EASILY. MANY
TIMES I GOT INTO FIGHTS – MOST
OF THE TIME, I LOST THESE FIGHTS.
THESE TEMPTATIONS LED ME TO
SELF-PITY, ANGER AND
RESENTMENTS. .

AS I GREW OLDER, I SUFFERED FROM DEPRESSION THAT ISOLATED ME FROM THE WORLD. I WAS TEMPTED AND SWORE AT GOD. I LASHED OUT AT MY PARENTS, PEERS AND TEACHERS.

BEFORE I ENTERED HIGH SCHOOL, MY WILL TOOK THE FORM OF ANGER AND I WAS OUT OF CONTROL. A PHYSICIAN PRESCRIBED VALIUM AND MY ADDICTION TO PRESCRIPTION DRUGS WAS LAUNCHED. DURING MY FRESHMAN YEAR, I GOT INTO FIGHTS AND BEGAN TO DRINK AT HOME. I BECAME DESPONDENT AND COULDN'T KEEP UP WITH MY SCHOOLWORK. (I DIDN'T KNOW AT

THIS TIME THAT I HAD A SEVERE HEARING LOSS.

AFTER HIGH SCHOOL, I GOT INVOLVED WITH WOMEN. THESE TEMPTATIONS SUCCEEDED IN LURING ME AWAY FROM GOD. I KNEW IT WAS WRONG, BUT NOTHING BAD HAPPENED. GOD DIDN'T CUT ME DOWN. I LOVED THE FLESH AND ITS VULNERABILITY.

OVER THE YEARS, I WOULD TEST MY FAITH THROUGH A SERIOUS ILLNESS, ALCOHOLISM, CANCER SCARE, BROKEN NECK, DEAFNESS, AND JOB LOSS THROUGH DISCRIMINATION. I BECAME

ANGRIER WITH GOD, BUT FOR
SOME REASON, NEVER STOPPED
PRAYING.

THROUGH THESE TRIALS, I
LEARNED ACCEPTANCE AND
TRUST. I SUFFERED GREATLY, BUT
THROUGH SURRENDERING MY
WILL, I TURNED EACH TRIAL INTO
MY STRENGTH. THE SUFFERING I
EXPERIENCED, THE LIFE
CHALLENGES I OVERCAME, HAVE
ALLOWED ME TO STAND TALL AND
HELP OTHERS.

AS I BECOME MORE SPIRITUALLY
HEALTHY, I AM ABLE TO LOVE AND
TRUST GOD. I SHARE THESE
STORIES WITH THOSE WHO ARE

LOST. I FELL FROM GRACE WITH GOD THROUGH MY SELFISHNESS. BY SHARING HONESTLY, I NOW WALK MORE IN GRACE AND SERENITY. MY UNHEALTHY DESIRES BROUGHT ME TO MY KNEES AND I LOOKED TO GOD FOR HELP. HE ANSWERED MY PLEA.

AS I PREPARE MY LIFE ON THIS EARTH FOR GOD AND WALK THIS SPIRITUAL PATH, I NEED TO REMAIN FAITHFUL AND READY EACH DAY TO SHARE MY SPIRITUAL MESSAGE WITH EVERYONE. THIS IS MY WALK IN LOVE, TRUST, FAITH AND OBEDIENCE THROUGH THE BIBLE'S TEACHINGS AND THE 12 STEPS OF ALCOHOLICS

ANONYMOUS...

CHAPTER 1

DISOBEDIENCE

SINCE I WAS DISOBEDIENT, I WANTED TO START THIS SECTION ON THE BIBLE'S VERSES ON DISOBEDIENCE AND HOW IT AFFECTED MY EARLIER LIFE.

IN GENESIS 3:21, THE VERY FIRST DEATH OCCURRED ON THE DAY AS ADAM AND EVE'S SIN; IT WAS THE DEATH OF AN ANIMAL TO PROVIDE A COVERING FOR THEIR NAKEDNESS. GOD'S IMMEDIATE PROVISION FOR SIN WAS THE SLAYING OF AN INNOCENT SUBSTITUTE TO PROVIDE SKINS TO CLOTHE THE GUILTY COUPLE. THE CLOTHING THEY WORE MUST HAVE

BEEN SERVED AS A REMINDER – ENGRAVING THE SIGHT OF THE DYING ANIMAL IN THEIR MINDS – A PICTURE OF THE TERRIBLE CONSEQUENCES OF THEIR SIN. AS WE RECOGNIZE THE SUFFERING, WE MAY HAVE CAUSED OTHERS; WE ALSO ARE REMINDED OF THE CONSEQUENCES OF REJECTING GOD'S PROGRAM OF LIFE.

IN GENESIS 4:6-7, WHEN GOD REJECTED CAIN'S OFFERING, CAIN REACTED WITH ANGER AND MALICE. GOD DID NOT REJECT CAIN FOR HIS STRONG FEELINGS, HE OFFERED HIM AN OPPORTUNITY TO START A NEW. IT IS SAD THAT CAIN REFUSED THIS

SECOND CHANCE AND INSTEAD WENT OUT TO KILL HIS BROTHER I NEED TO BE CAREFUL WHEN I FACED OBSTACLES IN MY RECOVERY PROGRAM. I NEED TO CAREFULLY WEIGH THE STRONG FEELINGS I ENCOUNTER WITHIN MYSELF BEFORE I ACT ON THEM. IF I DON'T, I MAY BE PASSING UP AN EXCELLENT OPPORTUNITY FOR A FRESH START. I KNOW THAT GOD IS NOT PUT OFF BY MY STRONG FEELINGS. RECOVERY IS BASED ON GOD'S LOVE THAT ALWAYS OFFERS ME AN OPPORTUNITY TO BEGIN AGAIN.

IN GENESIS 4:15, THE MARK OF

CAIN, WAS NOT, AS SOME HAVE TALKED A BADGE OF GUILT. GOD BANISHED CAIN FROM THE GROUND WITH HIS BROTHER'S BLOOD. IT WAS A SIGN THAT GOD GAVE TO CAIN FOR HIS PROTECTION. EVEN THOUGH CAIN FAILS GOD'S DESIRE TO PROTECT HIM FROM HARM. THE MIRACLE AND MARVEL OF THIS ACTION SHOWS HOW GOD PROTECTS US BEFORE I BEGAN MY RECOVERY. GOD YEARNS AND PROTECTS ME IN THE MIDST OF EVIL SO THAT I AM NOT DESTROYED. HE WANTS ONLY MY HEALING AND RECOVERY EVEN AFTER MY GREATEST FAILURES.

IN GENESIS 13:11:13, ONE BAD CHOICE LEADS TO ANOTHER. THE CHOICES WITH LOTS MADE IN THIS CHAPTER AND IN FOLLOWING CHAPTERS LEAD HIM TOWARD HIS EVENTUAL FALL. LOT CHOSE THE BEST LAND AND THE EASY LIFESTYLE THAT WOULD COME WITH IT. IN 13:12:13, LOT CHOSE TO MOVE CLOSER TO THE WICKED CITY OF SODOM. IN 19:1 – 18, HE CHOSE TO BECOME AN IMPORTANT MAN. IN IN A WICKED CITY. IN 19:30 – 38, LOT'S DESCENDANTS LEARNED OF LOT'S EVIL FIRST WHEN HE HAD HIS INCESTUOUS RELATIONS WITH HIS DAUGHTERS. I NEED TO THINK AHEAD, REFLECTING UPON THE PROBABLE CONSEQUENCES OF MY

PRESENT DECISIONS.

IN GENESIS 19:17 – 26, LOTS WIFE FAILED TO FOLLOW THE PROGRAM THAT THE ANGELS SET OUT FOR HER FAMILY. THE PLAN FOR THEM WAS TO RUN FROM SODOM AND NEVER LOOKED BACK... IT SPELLS HER DESTRUCTION IN THE PAST; I FOUND ATTEMPTING TO LOOK BACK AT MY DESTRUCTIVE SITUATIONS IN MY LIFE. THE FINAL EPISODE IN THE LIFE OF A LOST WIFE DEMONSTRATES THE FATAL CONSEQUENCES. IT'S OKAY FOR ME TO RUN, WITHOUT LOOKING BACK..

IN GENESIS 19:30 – 38, THE

INCEST AND LOTS FAMILY WAS A DIRECT RESULT OF LOT'S IRRESPONSIBLE DECISIONS IN THE PAST. LOT SPENT HIS YEARS IN A WICKED CITY AND FAILS TO FIND SUITABLE HUSBAND FOR HIS DAUGHTER. THEIR DESIRE FOR CHILDREN LED TO INCEST. THERE IS, HOWEVER, HOPE BEYOND THE SHOCKING DETAILS OF THE STORY. FURTHER RESEARCH INTO PETER 2:: 7- 8, STATES THAT MANY CENTURIES LATER THE APOSTLE PETER USED HIM AS A CLEAR EXAMPLE OF ONE WHOSE RIGHTEOUSNESS CAME BY GRACE THROUGH FAITH. LOT MOST DEFINITELY WAS A FLAWED PERSON, BUT GOD IS A GRACIOUS

GOD. THERE IS HOPE FOR ME, NO MATTER HOW BAD MY PAST ACTIVITIES MAY HAVE BEEN.

IN EXODUS, 21:12 – 27, THE COMMANDMENTS ARE DISCUSSED. THESE LAWS DEAL WITH THE CONSEQUENCES OF AN INAPPROPRIATE, ABUSIVE BEHAVIOR. IT IS INTERESTING TO NOTE THAT COMPENSATION FOR WRONG BEHAVIOR IS EMPHASIZED; MAKING IT CLEAR THAT GOD HOLDS ME ACCOUNTABLE FOR MY ACTIONS. THESE LAWS REVEAL GOD'S INSTRUCTIONS FOR MAINTAINING AN ORDERLY, HEALTHY SOCIETY WHEN PROPER BOUNDARIES HAVE BEEN

OVERSTEPED. THE COMMANDMENTS SAFEGUARD HUMAN RELATIONSHIPS AND PERSONAL IDENTITIES WHILE ALSO RECOGNIZING THE WORK OF LIFE AND PROPERTY.

IN GENESIS, 32:21 – 29: AARON REVEALS HIMSELF TO BE A PEOPLE PLEASER. AARON CAVED IN TO THE IDOLATROUS CRAVINGS OF THE ISRAELITES RATHER THAN CONFRONT THEM WITH THE SIN IN THEIR LIVES. AARON DISPLAYED A LACK OF HONESTY AND AN UNWILLINGNESS TO FACE THE REALITY OF HIS ACTIONS. AARON AVOIDED HIS ACCOUNTABILITY TO GOD AND MOSES BY MAKING A

FAR-FETCHED EXCUSE FOR HIS
BEHAVIOR, 32:22 – 24. THE
CONSEQUENCES OF HIS ACTIONS
WERE HORRIBLE, REACHING WAY
BEYOND HIS PERSONAL
REPRIMAND. I MUST DEFEND AND
LIVE OUT GOD'S PROGRAM, EVEN
WHEN IT'S UNPOPULAR WITH THE
CROWD. IF I DON'T, THE
CONSEQUENCES FOR THE PEOPLE
AROUND ME COULD BE TERRIBLE.

In Genesis 32:30 – 35, in the wake of the Levites killing around 3000 people, Moses took on the role of a father towards them in seeking atonement in forgiveness for the people since Moses asked God to hold back the terrible consequences. (A Great plague upon the people because they had worshiped the calf Aaron had made). Moses even suggested that he take the punishment upon himself. Unfortunately, God required that these disobedient people suffer the ultimate consequence – death.

In Leviticus, 26:14 – 39, God warns his people about what will happen to those who are disobedient to God's laws. They will suffer sudden terrors, with wasting disease with burning fevers. This long list of warnings goes on about the consequences of sin is really an extended love letter from God. God is not wanting us to suffer; he doesn't want to punish us. God does, however, understands the destructive consequences of sin. God knows that certain activities will cause suffering to me and to those around me. God warns the away from evil giving me a plan to follow that will lead to healthy and joyful living. God's program, who viewed by some as restrictive, is actually the shortest path to a life of fulfillment.

In Deuteronomy, 5:9 – 10, I learned that God is jealous of my affections, and when I fail to give him the proper place in my life, negative consequences always results. I am not the only one who will suffer so will my family. God created me to live according to his program. By limiting this program, I can have hope for my future. I need to start by putting God first in my life.

In Deuteronomy, 23:21 – 23, I learned that being trustworthy is an absolute necessity for anyone living God program. All enduring relationships are built on trust. When I make promises, I must keep them – even at great inconvenience to myself. For many people this is a problem. It breaks down relationships and eventually destroys them. I must realize that telling the truth is always best for me in the long run. The truth is one boundary I can never overstep without severe consequence. Those who disobey God's commandments will be cursed by God. Even negative passages like this remind me that God wants only my best. He wants me to obey because disobedience can only bring me suffering. This encourages me to follow God's path for healthy living.

In Deuteronomy, 28:66 – 67, these verses graphically draw a picture of life empty of happiness and satisfaction. This person dreads both night and day. When you are in the dark, he wishes for light. When it is light, he wishes for dark. This is the end results of rejecting God's plan for healthy living. There is no lasting satisfaction outside of a real relationship with God and obedience to his will. I need to see God's will and follow it without reservation.

It Judges 19:17 – 29, this tragic episode

represents the moral low point in Judges. There are powerful similarities between the Levites experiences with the Benjamites and Lot's experience with event of Sodom in Genesis 19. This experience is made worse because the uncaring Levite actually gave up his concubine to save his own skin and my son who fires the health and stability of my family so I would engage in this selfless lifestyle? If so, I need to accept the consequences of my actions. Levite blamed the Benjamites and did not recognize his responsibility in the tragedy by recognizing that I am accountable, I can't begin to get the assistance I need.

In Ruth 3:6 – 14, I enjoyed these verses since it is one of the great biblical examples of how the truth, clear personal boundaries and self-respect can protect people in compromising situations. Both Ruth and Boaz, no in a delicate a compromising situation, chose the right path. Both avoided the sexual gratification that many couples would have embraced; they refused to yield to live the chemistry and seduction of the moment. Ruth and Boaz considered the long term results of sexual activity outside the bounds of marriage. Boaz showed in unselfish love and concern for Ruth's safety 3:13 and her reputation. 3:14.

In one Samuel, 4:16 – 22, Eli and his family and indeed the entire nation of Israel, suffer the terrible consequences of disobedience. Eli and his sons died the arts of the covenant, the symbol of God's glorious presence with Israel, was captured by foreigners. The strong will remind me of how the refusal to abandon my shellfish, addictive lifestyle brings suffering upon my family and the people close to me. This point is illustrated in Eli's family by Eli's daughter in law. In her final words she named her baby Shabbat, meaning where is the glory? For: 21 – 22. Before her death, she acknowledged her hopelessness, but it was much too late for her and her family. Life recovery is not easy for it involves surrender, loss, pain and difficulty. The death of this young woman and the shattering of Eli's family should warn me about what is at stake if I do not persevere in my quest for recovery.

In first Samuel 5:6 – 12, the Philistines shows disrespect for the true God and suffered physical suffering as a direct consequence. The parallels today are unmistakable. By setting up addictions as gods in life, many people showed disrespect to the true God. They also violate God's laws by living selfishly and hurting people close to them. Those who violate God's standards experience physical repercussions. It is exactly this suffering that prompts them to seek help. So it was with the Philistines.

In first Samuel 6:19, the Lord kills 70 men from Beth-SHEMESH because they looked into the Ark of the Lord. This vaccine is like a harsh judgment, but it carries with it a reminder of the high cost of disobedience. The Israelites were held accountable to the instructions God had given them regarding the treatment of the ark they either ignored these instructions God had given them why they chose to ignore them. God, throughout the Bible, has given me instructions for healthy living. By failing to follow God's programs either from ignorance or choice, the consequences may be devastating. This group of Israelites neglected to follow God's instructions and the results was fatal. The same result may await me if I fail to listen to God and he and his word.

In 2nd Samuel, 5 – 13, David began to build his harem at the height of his political career. This practice was customary for Kings in the ancient near East, but his decision to be like other kings carried a price tag with it. The conflict between David and his children almost destroyed both. No moral judgment is cast here because polygamy was customary in Old Testament times. The consequences of family strife, however, are tested too numerous times in Scripture; many times God's plan will lead me away from the norms of the society around me. I have a choice. Either seek God's ideal or suffer the consequences.

And 2nd Samuel 6:1 – 8, David desired to bring the Ark of the Covenant, the symbol of God's presence to Jerusalem. However, he failed to follow God's specific instructions for transporting it. Most likely David never read God's law concerning the Ark, but God's word was available to him. God struck Luzon dead. The consequences were serious. I am responsible for knowing what God desires for me; this knowledge will enable me to act according to his will. The Bible is this source for knowing God's plan for healthy living.

In 2nd Samuel, 18:32 – 33, David could have avoided his sorrow, after Absalom's death, if he had been willing to forgive, get things straight, and restore his relationship with Absalom. David failed to seek reconciliation and now it was too late. He could never bring Absalom back nor could he even make things right with him. Reconciliation is important if I want to enjoy a peaceful future.

In Kings 2: 17 – 23, this chapter records the progressive degeneration of the northern kingdom of Israel leading to its destruction and exile. Hosea's reign was the straw that broke the camel's back. Hosea led Israel through its first climatic period of sinful denial, that ended in Assyrian exile. The nation of Judeo is criticized for making the same mistake, following the same evil path toward judgment and exile. Judah should have seen the consequences of Israel's disobedience and then pursue recovery. Like Judah, I need to be careful and head in the opposite direction of disaster. I must avoid Judah's terrible mistake:

In Chronicles 21:9 – 13, David was faced with a dilemma? All options open to him seemed to be bad. God offered him one. Three years of famine, to three months of destruction by Israeli as enemies, or 3 days of deadly plague. David chose the plague and 70,000 men died, but this alternative was the best choice. I pray that God delivers me from situations where all the options have severe consequences

In Chronicles 2:17, David was aware that the people of his kingdom would suffer for his personal sin. It's heartbreaking to read David submission of guilt as he accepted full responsibility for his sin. He then prayed diligently for the rescue of his people. When people close to me suffered because of my sins, I should pray that God would give them special space to overcome the consequences of my feelings.

In 2 Chronicles 12:5, I learned that turning from God has its consequences. Our Rehoboan had failed to lead his people in godly ways. As a result, they were abandoned by God. The prophet Shemaiah gave God's message in no uncertain terms. "You have abandoned me. So I am abandoning you".. Sin always brings destructive consequences. The most terrible consequences of all might be abandoned by God, without whom recovery is impossible. If I failed and sought forgiveness, however, God will help me deal with my past failures.

In 2 Chronicles 19: 1 – 2, the prophet chose Jehoshaphat to proclaim a message of judgment. Because of Jehoshaphat' S alliance what Ahab, he would have to bear the consequences. My allegiance needs to be with people who will encourage me and God program for recovery. Seeking help from anyone else will lead to negative consequences and suffering.

In Job 8:1 – 7, the expression, you get what you deserve, is perhaps the most unkind remark one can make to one who is suffering. Foolish choices often lead to painful consequences. But if I get when I deserved, I would soon be destroyed. Sometimes my suffering is not a consequence of sin. Bildad shows his ignorance of God's ways when he tried to conect Job's loss to some hidden sin. I know I need to be careful not to judge a person who is suffering a setback, for I may not know the whole story. God is the only one who knows and understands a person and his or her circumstances.

In Psalm 38, 1 – 8, God's judgment against my sinful habits may seem very harsh. His tough discipline, however, is intended for my good. Sin has consequences. God allows me to experience the painful results of my sentence in order to encourage me to turn to him. My suffering will only worsen unless I turn for my sins and commit my life to God. God is the only one who can help me overcome my sinful habits and reestablish my relationship. I would be wise to learn from my suffering rather than be destroyed by it.

In Psalm 60:1 – 4, God shows his anger because of my sins. I feel rejected and overwhelmed. At these times, I need to repent and renew my fellowship with Him. I know that the consequences of my sins and my mistakes often hurt others as well, and we ought to be sensitive to that fact and do my best to make the appropriate amends.

Discipline is never easy to take, but in the midst of it, God provide me with the direction I need to regain his favor and protection. God continues to reveal his program for spiritual recovery in his word.

In Psalm 88:6 – 12, in these verses the psalmist felt that God's anger waived heavily upon him. It is important to remember that God allows me to stumble and fall, giving me the opportunities to learn personally about the consequences of sin. God does not cause me to fall. Natural consequences are expected when I sin. If I am suffering because of my sins and failures, I should use the opportunity to learn from the past and turn to God.

In Proverbs 4:23 – 27, the warning to

guard my heart is also warning to not give in to the temptations of sinful pleasures of any kind. Indulging in sin is pleasurable at first, but in the end its promises are empty and bitter. Sin satisfies short term desires, but its consequences are long term. Returning to my addiction may make me feel better for the moment, but it will damage my program in the recovery process.

In Proverbs, 5:1 – 23, sexual temptation for me is easy for me to resist today. I'm well aware of the dangers and consequences of promiscuous sex. I know that sex outside of marriage is against God's law. Whether I am married or not. Throughout the book of Proverbs, there are warnings against promiscuity. Extramarital affairs can destroy family life and physical health and may result in pregnancy.

In Proverbs, 13:6, evil deeds destroy people and sin results in painful consequences. I know that alcohol will destroy my body and lying will ruin a person's reputation. To avoid the inevitable results of sinful behavior, I need to commit my life to the Lord, who's able to give me victory over my addiction and physical challenges. Proverbs teach me that God's way leads to happiness and gives positive direction to my life.

In Isaiah 8:6 – 8, Judah's leaders asked Assyrian for protection. This seems like a good solution at that time, but the long-term consequences are disastrous. The Assyrian armies eventually attack Judah and destroy the land. This attack could have been avoided had the leaders heeded God's warning. If my recovery program is based on anything other than God and his principles, I may wind up in greater peril later. Unlike Judah, I should seek a recovery plan that includes God.

Jeremiah 7:12, by examining the lives of those who have gone before me, I can see the blessings experienced by those who obey God and the terrible consequences of those who rebelled against him. Greed, denial, and pursuit of pleasure have destroyed the lives of many in my life. As I learned from those around me, I can make the changes I need to avoid their terrible fate.

In Jeremiah 21:1 – 14, a time comes

when it is too late to avoid the painful consequences of my actions. As Nebuchadnezzar bore down on Jerusalem, King Zedekiah wanted the persecuted prophet to petition God for help. God told them that it is too late. Since they had failed to respond to God's numerous warnings through his prophets, they endured enormous devastation. I would be wise to learn from my suffering rather than be destroyed by it.

In Psalm 60:1 – 4, God shows his anger because of my sins. I feel rejected and overwhelmed. At these times, I need to repent and renew my fellowship with him. I know that the consequences of my sins and mistakes often hurt others as well, and we ought to be sensitive to that effect and do my best to make the appropriate amends. Discipline is never easy to take, but in this the midst of it, God provides me with the direction I will need to regain his favor and protection. God continues to reveal his program for spiritual recovery in his word.

In Psalm 88:6 – 12, in these verses the psalmist felt that God's anger was heavily upon him. It is important to remember that God allows me to stumble and fall, given the opportunities to learn personally about the consequences of sin. God does not cause me to fall. Real consequences are expected when I'm in sin. If I am suffering because of my sins and failures, I should use the opportunity to learn from the past and then turn to God.

In Proverbs 4:23 – 27, the warning to guard my heart is also warning to not give in to the temptations of sinful pleasure of any kind. Indulging his sin is pleasurable at first but in the end its promises is empty and bitter sin satisfies short term desires, but it's consequences are long-term. Returning to my addiction may make me feel better for the moment, but it will damage my progress in my recovery process.

In in Proverbs, 5:1 – 23, sexual temptation is easy for me to resist today. I am well aware of the dangers and consequences promiscuous sex will bring. I know that sex outside of marriage is against God's law whether married or not. Throughout the book of Proverbs there are warnings against promiscuity. Extramarital affairs can destroy family life and physical health and may result in pregnancy.

In Proverbs 13:6, evil deeds destroy people and sin results in painful consequences. I know that alcohol will destroy my body and lying will ruin a person's reputation. To avoid the inevitable results of sinful behavior, I need to commit our life to the Lord, who's able to give me victory over my addiction and physical challenges. Proverbs teaches me that God's way leads to happiness and gives positive direction to my life.

In Jeremiah 25: 1 – 14, how impatient I become when the consequences of my sins last for days or weeks, much less years. The Israelites were captive under King

Nebuchadnezzar for 70 years. Many finally learned to honor God in the midst of captivity. Since their return from Babylonian captivity, the Jews have never been known to fall into sin of idolatry. It is important that I face the consequences of my behavior. One way we can honor God is to accept his discipline and build upon the lessons learned from sorrow.

In Lamentations 1:1 – 11, the sins of Judah's people led to the destruction and exile. This once prosperous nation fell to ruin. His capital city, was now silent, its beauty and majesty gone. The people felt abandoned by God. Jeremiah mourns the terrible losses. My sins also yield devastating consequences if I allow them to continue unchecked. If I am suffering terrible losses in my life, I should assess whether or not my sins have caused them. Recovery begins as mourn my losses and end my sins to God. If I do this, God can rebuild my life from the ruins.

In Ezekiel 5:8 – 10, God's judgment is righteous and cannot be avoided. Its inevitability and nature were answered by Ezekiel in detail. If I refuse to repent, I face God's judgment for my sins. The question is when, not if. Sin has terrible and unavoidable consequences. I cannot live the life that is out of control and hope to escape the consequences of my rebellion. God certainly loves me and wants me to restore me if I confess my sins to him and ask for his forgiveness. I cannot, however, do what I want whenever I want. God is just and will discipline his people when they continue to sin.

In Ezekiel 9:1 – 6, in Ezekiel's day, many Israelites believed they had nothing to fear because they had favored status of God's people. They thought that God was not blind to their sins. God was concerned about the people's blatant disregard for his laws, any way to make sure the offenders were punished. Sin always has consequences. God will not stand by idly and allow people to rebel against him forever. I must heed warnings and take appropriate action before it is too late.

In Ezekiel 21:3, the ominous words in this verse called Ezekiel to hold nothing back and express anguish at Jerusalem's coming destruction as a further warning to the people that Jerusalem's destruction was imminent. Uninhibited emotional expressions of this kind were normal in Israel. God would punish the entire nation, including a few good people. My sins always have consequences and very often those consequences are experienced by innocent people around us. My sins and dependency caused underserved pain for my spouse, friends, coworkers or employees. This pain has motivated me to seek changes in my life and make amends to those I have hurt.

In Ezekiel 39:1 – 6, I learned that every creature has to choose either to obey God or stand against Him. God had arranged his mighty forces against God's people; he had left God and his divine will out of the thinking altogether. God's destruction, promised by Ezekiel, reveals the consequences of choosing to stand against God and his will. When I see these terrible consequences, I am motivated to admit my own failures and take steps to follow God's will for my life.

In Ezekiel 44:6–7, refusing to obey God's will always bring painful consequences. God clearly revealed his will for his people but they refused to follow the guidelines. God had graciously provided. They rebelled against God's plan. God has clearly revealed his will for me in the Bible. It is my responsibility to follow it. Since there are consequences for failure to obey God's will, I would be smart to diligently seek God's will for my life and obey completely. If I take the steps, God will help me.

In Hosea 1:6, God seem to be saying that his relationship with Israel had ended. The naming Hosea's daughter Lo – Ruhamah show God's tough love. God had shown the Israelites mercy despite their unrepentant hearts. Now genuine love demanded that God take back that mercy to allow them to suffer the consequences of their actions and abandon all their false hopes. To see others experience the consequences of their actions is often hard to do because we don't want our loved ones to suffer, and I feel a sense of importance when I help them. The best thing to do for people who keep falling into sin is refuse to catch them so they can learn from the painful consequences of their actions and seek recovery.

And in Jonah 2:1 – 10, it took Jonah 3 days inside the fish to realize he would have to follow God's plan. God told Jonah to do something he didn't want to do. Jonah tried to do things his own way and suffer the consequences. I have similar choices. I can do things God's way and receive his help and blessing, or I can do things my way and suffer the painful consequences. God will go a long way to rescue his lost children and lead them back to Himself. In my own life, I had to hit rock bottom to realize that God's way is the only way.

To go back to Adam and Eve – there was an ideal situation a man and his wife living in harmony together in a lush, beautiful garden that God had created for their pleasure. They each enjoyed a perfect relationship with God and with each other. But when Adam's needs gave into temptation, they overstepped their God – given boundaries and plans for humanity into sin. Shame and guilt penetrated their lives and created an invisible barrier between them and God. The results were their sins and lack of self.

And even when against God's – plan. A plan that was created with their best interests in mind. The consequences of their sin followed immediately. They became afraid of the God who loved them so much.. They became ashamed of their nakedness and set out to cover themselves. Their relationship cracked. Accusations were made. Blame was shifted. Neither wanted to be held accountable. Both of them refuse to admit that they were wrong. Needless to say, their relationship was damaged. Their sin separated them from each other and from God.

Jacob's family and sons, while not the first dysfunctional family in the Bible. Jacob's breed was certainly among the most controversial. Like father, like son, the saying goes, that Jacob's own lack of discretion, honesty patience and unconditional love impacted his family negatively.

Jacob was not his father's favorite, and he played favorites with his sons with tragic results. Joseph was his favorite with Benjamin running a close second. The rest were far back in the pack and understandably jealous.

The deceptions that Jacob put over on his father and brother in earlier years were married in the lies son told about Joseph's fate. Openness and honesty didn't characterize the sons relationships with outsiders either. Jacob's silence at Dinah's grave perhaps spurred Simeon and Levi to seek vengeance.. Certainly their fathers set no clear boundaries on their behavior until it was much too late.

Jacob's polygamy also influenced his sons. Reuben had grown up watching the marital triangle expand to include two servants' concubines. Reuben had even been a party to his mother's and Rachel's rivalry for Jacobs favors. He was not the only one to sin sexually. Judah succumbed to temptation with his daughter in law, Tamara.

Jacob and his sons did mature significantly over the years. Famine forced them to visit Egypt. When this happened, they were no longer the selfish, jealous and deceitful bands of earlier years. Instead, they were generally concerned about their aging father, protective of young Benjamin and remorseful when confronted with the truth of what they had done to Joseph. They reconciled their past and began an exciting new life in Egypt with the brother they once abandoned. They became worthy to become the forefathers of Israel's 12 tribes. Judah even had the royal line, with the descendants the King of Kings, Jesus Christ.

In David, Michal, and Bathsheba in Samuel 6 – 16, David failed in many of his relationships. He avoided conflict and therefore did not deal with some important issues in his life. His first wife, Michal, was a daughter of King Saul. Their marriage was right out of a fairytale. The King's daughter married the one-time shepherd boy who became a Great War hero. He was also the most talented musician of his day. Their relationship appeared to be fine, but over time difficulties develop. She was separated from David for a few years when Saul gave her to another man spite David. David later won her back but brought her back into his home filled with his other wives. Their relationship was never the same after Michal's return.

Michal exploded at David for dancing before the Ark as David celebrated his return to Jerusalem 6:16. Her bitterness and frustration over the years of separation and neglect have built to the boiling point. It appears there was no indication that they ever tried to heal their damage marriage relationship. They settled into destructive silence.

David's life became more complicated by his infatuation and adultery with by Bathsheba 11:1 – 27. His sin led to a tangled web of deceit involving Uriah murdered. His sin also involves him in a rushed marriage to the pregnant Bathsheba.

This trail of self-induced tragedies left a cloud of shame that hung over David for the rest of his life. Unfortunately, David's own children repeated his mistakes, bringing further suffering to the royal family and the nation as a whole.

David was considered more righteous than Saul his predecessor. His heart was open before God, and he was willing to accept god's correction in his life. With each failure, he was willing to admit to the truth, except the consequences, and receive God's forgiveness. Even in the midst of his failures, pain, and grief, David remains a man whose primary desire was to know God. Like David, I have made mistakes. I have learned a lot from him about recovering from the bad choices I have made.

In 2 Samuel 12 – 14, the tragic example of Ammon and Tamar breaking God's laws about sexual behavior brought devastation into their lives.

Ammon was David's oldest son, and Tamar was Ammon's half-sister. He nurtured this fantasy until he shared it with a cousin. Ammon chose to satisfy his desire and raped Tamar. He became blind to the consequences that were soon to follow.

Tamar was violated, abandoned and changed. Ammon's actions cost Tamar the honorable future expected for a King's Daughter. When Absalom, Tamara's brother, learned of Tamar's rape, he was filled with rage and killed Ammon. Some of the consequences of Amnon's sin caused Tamara to lose her purity, Ammon losing his life, and David losing his son.

David was the head of a dysfunctional family. He failed to confront Ammon about his sin. Speculation has it that David had failed by committing sexual sin with Bathsheba. Tamar's family responded to the crisis with silence, deception, rage and denial. The sin of Ammon had terrible consequences and Davis failures to deal with that sin only compounded the devastation.

Jeremiah was born into a priestly clan and was called into the prophetic ministry as a youth. In spite of his age, Jeremiah was humble and eager to serve God. His ministry stretched from the 13th year of King Josiah's reign until after Jerusalem's destruction.

Josiah's reign was the last highpoint in Judah's spiritual history and Jerusalem was an ally in the King's reforms. When Josiah died, Judah quickly declined spiritually causing great distress to Jerusalem. He continued to preach against the hypocrisy and corruption of prophets, priests and government officials alike. He foretold that the nation faced sure destruction because of its sins – a message that few believed. The people wanted to believe the false prophets who predicted a rosy future for Judah.

Jeremiah was the victim of intense persecution. He was thrown into dungeons, beaten, put into irons, threatened and almost killed. Some biblical tradition states that he was eventually stoned to death. Jeremiah remained a man of prayer and deep spirituality, and he faced trials with courage. He faced much opposition, but remain true to the word God had given him. He confronted the Jews with their denial and encouraged them to admit their sins and asked God for forgiveness. He spoke words of comfort to the people facing disaster.

Jeremiah was honest about how he felt. He is known as the weeping prophet. He shed tears not from his own suffering but for his people who sin repeatedly and would not repent.

When Jerusalem was destroyed and

people exiled, Jeremiah wept for the pain and loss of this people who suffered. Jeremiah spoke openly and honestly and complained to God about the work God had given him to do. Yet even in the midst of his depression, Jeremiah never lost faith in God – power to judge righteously, to reward liberally, and restore his broken and sinful people.

In Nehemiah 9:1 – 3, I learned a valuable lesson about step 4 in recovery. By making a moral inventory of myself, I find myself listing my destructive habits, defects of character and the wrongs I have done. Also, the consequences of wrong choices. I know I lived with the pain in my heart that I caused others. The process is like sifting through all the garbage in my past. It is a painful process, but necessary to rid the rotten habits and behaviors that will spoil the rest of my life.

The return of the Jewish exiles allowed them to confess their own sins. Confession means owning up to one sins in being truly sorry for them as well. The Israelites confession serves as a model for me to follow as I take my moral inventory. I list all the occasions of my offenses, my destructive habits, and the consequences I have brought into my life and the lives of others.

In their confession, Israelites owned, bemoaned and discarded their sins. When they finished, they were better able to make a new start. I can own the garbage in my own life by taking personal responsibility for my choices and actions. I can bemoan it by allowing myself to grieve. I can discard by leaving it behind and turning toward the future.

In Galatians 6:7 – 10, I learned that I'm a fool myself in believing that I can simply bury my wrongs and go on without needing to admit them. In time, I actually found that these deeds I thought I'd buried once and for all were actually seeds. They grew more fruit. Eventually, I had to deal with the harvest of consequences and face the fact that self-deception doesn't work to my advantage.

I want to quote to verses from Galatians 6:7 –8," You will always reap what you sow! Those who live only to satisfy their own sinful desires will harvest the consequences of decay and death. But those who live to please the Spirit will harvest everlasting life from the spirit".

I need to say goodbye to self-deception and hello to forgiveness and cleansing. There is a cleansing from every wrong. Admitting the exact nature of my wrongs and accepting the consequences of my wrongs includes giving my accounts in exact and specific terms. When I get specific, I am no longer able to fool myself about the nature of my wrongs. I cannot ignore God and get away with it anyway. I must come clean and be forgiven

Another consequence of recovery is accountability. I learned to accept responsibility for my actions. These actions yield consequences. I cannot escape the consequences of the bad choices I made. It is clear that God has made accountability a necessary element of healthy living.

The law of sowing and reaping can also work to our benefit. In Hosea 10:12, God spoke through Hosea saying," plant the good season righteousness, and you will harvest a crop of my love. Plow up the hard ground of your hearts, for now is the time to seek the Lord, that he may come and shower righteousness upon you."

Even after I have been forgiven, I must deal with consequences of my actions. I know it will take time to finish harvesting the negative consequences of my past, but this need not discourage me.

I would like to comment with a segment from Revelation 20:11 – 15 on God's mercy. The day will come when I will have to face the truth about myself and my life.

The book of Revelation tells me there is a day coming when inventory was made of every life.

It is wise for me now to do my earthly moral inventory so I can be ready for Jesus' coming. Anyone whose name is in the book of life will be saved, including all whose sins have been atoned for by the death of Jesus. Those who refuse God's offer of mercy are left judged on the basis of their own deeds recorded in" the books". No one is going to pass that test. Now is a good time to make sure that my name is in the right book. Knowing that my sins are covered with God's forgiveness can help me examine my life fearlessly and honestly.

CHAPTER 3

Love

Ephesians 1:4 - "Long ago, even before he made the world, God loved me and chose me in Christ to be holy and without fault in His eyes"

How can I have confidence that God will hear my prayers? How do I know he will answer when I ask him to remove my shortcomings and forgive my sins?

The apostle Paul wrote that God's primary goal is to make me holy, which is, to form his character in me.

My eyes are the windows to my spirit. Love is the core of all Bible teachings. When I look through the eyes of love, God already sees me, as I will be when his work is done.

In Genesis 30:25-43, God always treated Jacob in ways far better than he deserved. God blessed him in spite of his trickery and deceit. God works that way with me, also. He is willing to bless me with healing even when I don't really deserve it. I don't really deserve God's love. I have failed in many ways. God reaches out to help me when I look to him in faith.

In Exodus 11:9-10, God gave Pharaoh numerous chances to go after his heart. The tough love God used in this progression of plagues eventually led the King to hit bottom emotionally. God often intervenes in my life in similar ways. When difficult times arise, I may become angry with God. It might be smart for me to start listening. God might be giving me chances to find a new life. He uses the difficulties I face to show me my errors and lead me to correct my ways. I can't refuse God's intervention. I need to learn from God's hard lessons, realizing his spirit will help me through all my difficulties and pain.

In Exodus 20:1-11, the first four commandments provided the Israelites with a few foundational principles to govern their relationships with God. They were not to worship any other gods, make idols of any kind or misuse God's name. They were also to remember to observe God's Sabbath day of rest. Jesus later summed up this vertical relationship as the greatest commandment.

"You must love the Lord your God with all your heart, all your soul and all you mind." (Matthew 22:37). Loving God means I need to live out a consistent faith and commitment to him.

In Exodus 21:-12-17, the final four commandments deal with principles that define boundaries for healthy human relationships. Jesus summed up these human relational boundaries like this. "Love you neighbor as yourself." (Matthew 22:39). This great commandment assumes that I have cultivated a healthy self-respect and follow it up with loving actions that respect the boundaries of others.

In Deuteronomy 6:5, the Israelites were told to love God with all their heart, soul and strength. Jesus called this the most important commandment in the Bible. If I love God, I will want to do everything he asks. The nature of this love, however, is often misunderstood. In the Bible, love is not primarily an emotion. Love is a decision that shows itself in appropriate actions. Hence, loving God entails following God's program, looking to him constantly for help and forgiveness.

In Deuteronomy 11:1, my obedience to God's instructions should be a direct result of my love for him. My love for God is the major motivating force in my obedience to the civil, ceremonial and moral obligations he requests to me. My love is a natural response to the love he has shown me.

In 2 Samuel 13:14-16, Amnon's selfish lust brought terrible consequences. Tamar's future was destroyed and her hope's for a good marriage were dashed. Amnon lived with his guilt and he soon would be murdered for his actions. Amnon also discovered the bitter taste of sexual activity, driven by selfish desire. His self-centered love turned to hate. I cannot use lust as love because it will ruin this special gift given to me by God.

In Psalm 73:21-29, this psalmist began to think that God was unjust and he had a hard time believing that God loved him. God was waiting to restore his relationship with the doubting psalmist. I need God's help if I want to succeed in recovery. Like the psalmist, I need to realize that God does love me and that his plan for me is the best, if I trust in God, and seek to follow his will for me, he will keep guiding me with good counsel. .

In Psalm 99:1-9, even though I know that God is a God of love, he is also holy and righteous. God's love causes him to show mercy toward me, but his holiness means that I can't please him if I continue in sin. I must not presume God's love and forgiving nature, for God also loves justice. If I resort again to sin, the result will be terrible consequences. God's delivering power should motivate me to live for him with all my strength.

In Psalm 103:13-18, a loving father cares for his children. God has compassion on all who call on him. He is sensitive to my needs and treats me lovingly because he understands my weaknesses and the transitory nature of my life. By obediently serving God now, I can be assured that his love will touch not only my own life, but also the lives of my own ones.

In Proverbs 3:11-12, when God disciplines me, he is not doing so because he hates me or wants me to suffer. He is correcting me because he loves me and doesn't want me to go any further into my sin. To help me see the true nature of God, I need to look to the Gospels and examine the love Jesus had for others. When I understand that Jesus and God are one and the same, I can more readily accept that God loves me and has my best interests in mind as he disciplines me.

In Song of Songs 7:1-9, Solomon's praise of his bride continues. As the couple matured in their love, the passion did not diminish. It shows that passionate love can last as a marriage matures. In my marriage, the passion diminished because both of us didn't mature spiritually. I wish I had the opportunity to assess my wrongs with her and the possibility of reconciliation and stability.

In Jeremiah 18:12-15, the people of Judah were aware of their sins and even admitted them openly, yet stubbornly refused to change. God's only recourse was to destroy Israel and the exile of his people. His love led him to punish them in hope that they would finally respond with repentance. Admission without change is meaningless. The more I know about myself, the greater my responsibility to change what I know needs changing.

In Jeremiah 23:1-4, shepherds are the leaders of God's people. They are supposed to care for God's "sheep" that had scattered and forsaken them. Judah's leaders led God's people astray. God promised to punish the leaders and gather his people. He vowed to place them in the care of responsible shepherds who would love and tend them. Jesus is my good shepherd, loving me and tending to me as his flock. I am willing to seek and follow his will for my life. There is hope for me, no matter how far I may have strayed.

In Jeremiah 44:1-30, God is worthy of my love and obedience; whether or not he gives me what I want. God can be trusted at the deepest level. His plan for my life is always best. Jeremiah encouraged the remnant in Egypt to learn from Judah's recent fall and to turn away from idolatry. Sadly their love for God was conditional. Unless God rewarded them in the ways they expected, they would not obey them.

In Lamentations 2:1-18, God's anger is motivated by his love. Anger is his last resort as he seeks to get my attention. God's purpose is not to destroy but to bring repentance and restoration to my life. In these verses, there are devastating consequences of his anger. God is always slow to anger and quick to forgive. The Israelites were warned of the disaster by God's prophets for centuries before their enemies finally destroyed the holy city of Jerusalem.

In Lamentations 3:27-39, God shows me that He disciplines me because he loves me. When I follow a dangerous path, I need to be stopped. Sometimes the only way God can get my attention is by knocking me down. I may get angry with God for his discipline, but it is definitely an opportunity for change. I take a moral inventory to discover the root of my problems and then turn my problems and sins over to God and seek to live according to his ill.

In Hosea 3:1-2, Hosea was able to heal

his broken family by redeeming, or buying back, his wife Gomer, that highlights his extraordinary love for her. She did not come back to him so he went to her and paid more to buy her back. This symbolizes God's love that is still even more extraordinary.

In Zechariah 3:16-17, it's pointed out that after Jesus' Baptism, the Holy Spirit was seen in visible form, and the Father commended his Son. Jesus is thus shown to be perfect harmony with his Father and the Holy Spirit. As I study the Bible, God's love letter to the human race, I see many examples of God's unlimited love for me. Knowing how much my heavenly Father loves me can help offset the lack of love and affirmation from my earthly relationships.

In Matthew 5:43-48, when I love my enemies, I can be sure that I am making progress in my in my spiritual walk. Loving my enemies doesn't mean I have to like them, but it does mean I must forgive them in love and desire what is best for them. God loves me even though I am far from perfect. My recovery is not perfect. My walk is the ability to follow God and shape my decisions and actions according to his will for me.

In Matthew 22:33-40, Jesus narrowed the six hundred regulations of the Law of Moses into two fundamental commandments. Love God with everything I am and have and love my neighbors as ourselves. When I love God with my very life, I will not want to do anything to disgrace Him or make him angry. Loving others makes me aware of the pain others feel when I engaged in my past. My love for them makes me think twice before causing them to suffer.

In Mark 12:28-34, some think of religion with all the commandments as a straightjacket, a paradox to recovery and spiritual growth. Jesus wanted to correct this false understanding of true faith. He summed up the numerous Jewish laws in two simple but profound commandments – love God totally and loves others as much as I love myself. If these two thoughts rule my heart and mind, I will be well along the path toward spiritual recovery.

In Luke 10:25-37, the story of the Good Samaritan teaches me that true love for God expresses itself in caring for other's needs. In Jesus' day, the Jews and Samaritan hated one another. When the despised Samaritans proved to be the good neighbor to the wounded Jew, Jesus was showing that concern for others has no boundaries. God has brought me healing and spiritual recovery. As a result, I'm becoming an effective instrument in reaching others with similar needs. Sharing God's good news of my deliverance is a responsibility I receive from God. As I share, I will experience great joy as others gain hope for recovery. My own faith and walk are strengthened as I remember what God has done on my behalf.

In John 13:34-35, I learned my ability to love others and myself is based on the degree to which I have received God's love. When I try to love others without God's love, I try to give what I don't have. Many times I ended up giving to others in hopes of receiving something in return. This selfish act never feels good to me or to the person I am trying to help. When I love someone out of the overflow of God's love, my witness and service can be effective toward my spiritual recovery.

In John 19:28-30, I asked what did Jesus finish? On the cross, Jesus finished the work he was sent to do and paid for my sins. In the greatest act of love in history and to fulfill a complicated, centuries old system of sacrifices, he became the perfect sacrificial Lamb of God. The miracle of the Resurrection confirmed that Jesus is the

Savior who can bring salvation and forgiveness, new life and spiritual recovery to me.

In Romans 8:31-39, Paul writes my security in life and in spiritual recovery is based on God's unshakable love for me. The love God has for me is not just an emotion but also a matter of historical record. God proved his love for me by sending His Son to suffer and die. There is nothing in the whole universe that can separate me from God's love!

In Romans 12:9-21, God tells me to let love govern all my attitudes and actions. This definitely applies to the process of spiritual recovery. I am even called to love my enemies. I been wronged by others and

God's love allows me to forgive them and seek reconciliation. Others hurt me. Love enables me to ask for their forgiveness and seek to make amends for the trouble and pain I have caused. I need to make an effort to reach out to certain people. Love in action is not easy. It demands that I swallow my pride and admit my wrongs to others. As painful as love may be, however, it is the only way to experience the joy of relationships and progressing in my walk.

In Romans 13:8-10, Paul says that my spiritual recovery can only take place when I learn to love others. Love is not an emotion I feel. Love is an attitude and outpouring of unselfish concern for others. When I love God and the people around me, I will treat others with respect. I will not steal from or harm anyone in any way to satisfy my own selfish desires. As I continue to examine myself, I use love as the standard by which I judge my behavior. Do I act with the best standard by which I judge my behavior? Do I act with the best interests of others in mind? When I measure all my actions against God's standard of love, I will experience great progress in recovery and in my relationships.

In I Corinthians 8: 1-3, love is shown as a lifestyle where my thoughts and actions are guided by my concern for others. I need spiritual recovery because I have lived for my own gratification. Through my addiction and physical challenges, I became blind or oblivious to the needs of the people around me. A life governed by selfless love is the only path to rebuilding my broken past. Knowing that God loves me no matter what my past, is the start of my spiritual journey.

Love brings security into my life. For me, the feelings of insecurity contribute to the power of my dependency. Believing that love can bring lasting security may be difficult for me because I experienced abandonment, abuse, addiction and physical challenges. Jesus promised in John 14:18, "No, I will not abandon you as orphans – I will come to you." I have asked myself many times how can I trust in God's love when it feels like all I've ever known is love that disappoints? In Psalm 103:14-18, the psalmist writes, "For he understands how weak we are; he knows we are only dust…The wind blows, and we are gone…but the love of the Lord remains forever with those who fear him."

God's love is unconditional and always waiting for me. Turning my life over to God involves opening the door of my heart to his love. Filling upon God's love will help me to deal with my physical challenges and to avoid spiritual relapses. His love meets me at my deepest need and overcomes my most powerful insecurities.

In Corinthians 13:11-13, I learned that genuine love is the greatest healer of all. My recovery and spiritual growth are never completed in this life. When I see God face to face I will be complete and whole. Paul shared this truth not to discourage me, but to give me hope that someday, I will be made perfect. I need to persevere in my spiritual journey and have faith in God and those around me. I need hope to endure and be healed from my painful problems and physical challenges. I need genuine love to conquer the barriers and bondage of my past. Faith, hope and love are all necessary in my spiritual walk.

In Galatians 5:22-24, love, joy, patience, kindness, goodness, faithfulness, gentleness and self-control are qualities produced by the Holy Spirit's work in a life submitted to God. As a tree bears fruit by means of God's silent work in nature, I experience fruits of the Spirit by means of God's power alone. My role is to entrust my life to him.

As the Holy Spirit begins to bear these fruits in my life, my dependency loses its power. Joy and peace overcame the pain of my broken past. With love, kindness, goodness, faithfulness and gentleness, I restore my relationships and make amends, with patience, I preserve through the difficult times. God's Spirit can supply everything necessary for a successful spiritual recovery

In Ephesians 3:14-21, I learned that through God healing is possible. When I'm grounded in God's love, spiritual recovery will follow. Paul wrote these verses that for churches or small groups to function effectively as vehicles for spiritual growth, the need to be driven by God's dynamic and unlimited love. Paul prayed that his friends might be deeply anchored and rooted in the soil of God's love. As I learn how much God loves me, I will become confident that he is able to do far more in and through me than I could ever imagine.

In Philippians 2: 1-4, I'm reminded that I am never an island unto myself. I am part of a whole, a member of Christ's body. As a member of a loving community, when others hurt – I hurt. When I hurt, others hurt. As I grow beyond self- centeredness, I become interested in others. . As I love others, I find that others will love me.

In Titus 2:11-15, I realize how much God loves me and that he provides the power for me to live a godly life. As a result, I am motivated to entrust my life to him and seek his will. God loves me and desires to help me succeed. God is accepting, gracious and compassionate instead of harsh, condemning, and punitive. God loves me and will help me rebuild my life when I admit my failures to him. This gives me hope as I grow through my spiritual walk.

In Peter 2:2-3, in these verses Peter pinpointed an insight for helping me resist sin and continue to walk in love for God. I can live a godly life because I have tasted God's kindness. When I experience God's love, I won't want to sin because I will see that it is not good for me. Sin grieves God's Spirit. This puts the focus in my spiritual recovery walk on improving outward behavior, but on seeking to please God and experience more of his kindness. I can come to him with all of my needs, and he will fill my heart with the love I crave.

In 1 John 21:7-11, John writes about another distinctive mark of my faith – loving others. I know that hatred towards others is a sign that spiritual recovery has not begun. Light and darkness cannot exist in the same heart. The absence of love will keep me in the dark and prove a severe hindrance to progress in my spiritual walk. Love is never weak or compromising. Love is the evidence of emotional strength. The love God gives me provides the energy to approach those I have harmed and to make amends when possible.

In 1 John 3: 10-20, John uses Cain and Abel as examples. John under scored the importance of love. The best way to express my love for God is the willingness to make sacrifices for the ones I love. My actions toward others, not just my words, reveal what's in my heart.

In 1 John 4:7-12, John points out that the Father's love for me is substantial enough to have sent his Son to save me. As I grow to be more like him, I also grow in my ability to love others with sacrificial love. Many times I feel my spiritual walk would be greatly expedited if only I could see God. God, however, is usually seen only through his people when they love one another. It is so important for me to restore my relationships with the people I have harmed. That is the reason I need the fellowship of believers – because I desperately need the love they offer.

In 1 John 4:16-23, John spoke again about the importance of love. True Christianity is characterized by loving relationship in which there is no fear. Experiencing these relationships – first with God, then with other believers – is at the heart of spiritual recovery. Where love reigns, I can be open and vulnerable with fellow believers, trusting that my honesty will not be used to hurt me. Helping others creates an environment where I develop accountability and a new sense of responsibility towards others and myself.

In Deuteronomy 30:15-20, God spoke through Moses, saying, "Now listen. Today, I am giving you a choice between prosperity and disaster, between life and death. I have commanded you today to love the Lord your God and to keep his commands, laws and regulations by walking in his ways. If you do this, you will live…and the Lord your God will bless you…. Choose to love the Lord your God and to obey him and commit yourself to him, for he is your life." I have chosen to set my heart in the direction of life and love. I can and have chosen to love God and begin to follow his ways.

Hosea was a prophet to the rebellion nation of Israel. God used Hosea's life to demonstrate his unconditional love for his people and me. The Lord told Hosea to marry a prostitute. Hosea married her, loved her, and devoted himself to her. His wife later relapsed into her old ways, broke Hosea's heart, and brought shame on their family. She fell into slavery. God then baffled Hosea by telling him, "Go and get your wife again. Bring her back to you and love her, even though she loves adultery. For the Lord still loves Israel even though the people have turned to other gods. "(Hosea 3:1)

I many times ask how God could still love me. But God asks, "Oh, how can I give you up…? How can I let go? How can I destroy you…? My heart is torn within me, and my compassion overflows, for I am God and not a mere mortal. I am the Holy One living among you, and I will not come to destroy." Hosea (11:8-9) there is absolutely nothing I can do or confess to

God that would cause him to stop loving me.

My profound hearing loss and other physical challenges have led to loneliness and isolation even when I am around other people. I feel guilt, fear of being hurt, abandoned and unable to believe in the love others have for me. I feel all alone in my struggle even when there are people beside me who want help.

Loneliness can break me and defeat me in my spiritual walk. Help is available and I need to prepare my heart to accept whatever love, support or friendship is offered in return. These supportive relationships, along with God's supporting hand, will strengthen my life considerably.

Wise King Solomon observed, "Two people can accomplish more than twice as much as one, they get a better return for their labor. If one person falls, the other can reach out and help. But people who are alone when they fall are in real trouble. And on a cold night two under the same blanket can gain warmth from each. But how can one be warm alone? A person standing alone can be attacked and defeated, but two can stand back to back and conquer. Three are even better, for a triple braided card is not easily broken." (Ecclesiastes 4:9-12)

With my friends and God joining with me to form a "triple braided card", I will not be easily broken or turned from my spiritual path.

Paul wrote in Romans 5:3-5, "We can rejoice, too, when we can run into problems and trials, for we know that they are good for us – they help us learn to endure. And endurance develops strength of character in us, and character strengthens our confident expectations of salvation…for we know how dearly God loves us, because he has given us the Holy Spirit to fill our hearts with his love."

Learning to wait patiently is an important characteristic for me to develop. Each time I admit my importance and accept God's forgiveness, my faith and hope grow stronger. God's love for me is reaffirmed every time. I rely on it. In this manner, God helps me hold my head high no matter what happens.

When touching on deep sensitive issues in my life, it is important to speak in the language of love, not condemnation. In Galatians 6:1-2, the Bible tells me that if someone, "is overcome by some sin, you who are godly should gently and humbly help that person back onto the right path. And be careful not to fall into the same temptation yourself. Share each other's troubles and problems and in this way obey the laws of Christ." The command was the one Jesus taught his disciples. "So now I am giving you a new commandment: Love each other. Just as I have loved you, you should love each other". John 13:34. In John 15:12-13, John says, "I command you to love each other in the same way that I love you. And here is how to measure it – the greatest love is shown when people lay down their lives for their friends."

I can love others as he loved me. Love goes beyond mere words. Sometimes it is spoken in silence, when I don't condemn someone who comes to me looking for help. Love doesn't just tell them what the problems are. Love carries the weight of their burdens. My support network helps me until I am able to take steps toward my spiritual walk on my own initiative.

In Ruth, 2:4-18, "Please love me." This is the whispered cry of my heart. I may not want to admit it for fear of rejection, but I am hungry for love. I know I am starving for affection because of previous losses.

Ruth was a young woman who had

known loss and hunger. Her husband died, leaving her without any means of emotional or physical sustenance. She accompanied her mother-in-law Naomi to a foreign land and gathered leftover grain from harvested fields just to have enough to stay alive. Boaz, the man who owned the fields, was a relative who could marry Ruth if he chose, and fulfill her needs for love and protection. Naomi instructed her to go to the threshing floor where Boaz was sleeping and curl up at his feet. Culturally, this displayed a request to be taken care of. Boaz was quite happy to find Ruth there and later married her, providing the love and provision she had lost and longed for.

As I turn my life over to God, I need to venture toward developing healthy love relationships with people and with God. I know it's scary to say, "Please love me", but it's worth the risk. If I don't satisfy my hunger for love in a legitimate way, I will be driven back toward depression. I know when I "curl up" at the feet of Jesus, he will be glad to find me there. He will provide for me, protect me, and love me.

I previously wrote about Hosea, but wish to expound on this story here. God told the prophet Hosea to marry a prostitute. His marriage became a living example to the nation of Israel of its infidelity toward God. It hurt Hosea deeply when his wife returned to her life of prostitution. Hosea said, "Then the Lord said to me, 'Go and get your wife again. Bring her back to you and love her, even though she loves adultery.

For the Lord still loves Israel even though the people have turned to other gods, of offering them choice gifts.' So I brought her back for fifteen pieces of silver and about five bushels of barley and a measure of wine. Then, I said to her, 'you must live in my house for many days and stop your prostitution. During this time, you will not have sexual intercourse with anyone, not even with me.'" Hosea 3: 1-3

Hosea needed time before he could be close to his wife again. Sometimes the best way I can make amends to my ex-wife is allow time to pass. My physical challenges caused my marriage to fail. I finally spoke with her after many years and made my amends.

There were times in my life when I loved people and yet hurt them. This paradox caused shame and sometimes created barriers between the ones I loved and me.

Peter once swore his love for Jesus. But after Jesus was arrested, Peter protected himself by denying that he even knew Jesus. Jesus wasn't surprised, but Peter had a hard time forgiving himself. After Jesus rose from the dead, he spoke with Simon Peter, 'Simon son of John, do you love me more than these? 'Yes, Lord', Peter replied, 'Yes know I love you'…Once more he asked him, 'Simon son of John, do you love me? Pete was grieved that Jesus asked the question a third time. He said, 'Lord you know everything   you know I love you,'" John 21:15-17

Jesus allowed Peter to affirm his love the best he could and accepted Peter as he was. In this way, Jesus reduced the shame and restored the relationship. Shame and isolation can lead me back to my old ways. I must not allow my isolation to separate me and avoid the people I love. I know I love others imperfectly. No one is perfect. I, however, need to keep my love relationships together until I have had time to heal.

In my past, I have felt that love doesn't seem to work for me. I sometimes wonder if I am doing something wrong. It is possible. I had problems loving because I was disconnected from the source of true love.

The apostle John wrote, "Dear friends,

let us continue to love one another, for love comes from God…But anyone who does not love does not know God – for God is love." John 4:7-8.

Chapter 4

Faith

Faith is the key that unlocks the door to successfully work my spiritual recovery and believe in God. I cannot afford to stand back, hoping for "cures", and avoid deliberate action because of my lack of faith. I can come to believe in God, and have the faith to take hold of my own recovery. As a result, I will find the healing power I have been looking for -Jesus Christ.

In Genesis 12:1, I learned that a relationship with God is a two way street. He is there to help me, but he expects me to follow his plan. When God called Abram to leave his country and his people and go to a land that God would show him, God promised to guide him. Abram, however, had to step out in faith. God has promised to be with me as I seek his help in spiritual recovery and with my physical challenges, but he may also ask something of me. As with Abram, God may call me away from the familiar world that drags me down. If I want to progress, I will need to follow his plan.

In Genesis 15:6, this verse is one of the most important in the Old Testament. Abram believed God, and God declared him righteous. It was Abram's faith, not his works that made him righteous before God. I need to trust God more and trust my works less. I am powerless over the pressures of sin, but God will help me through the toughest temptations if I trust him. He will count me righteous because of my trust in him, not because I am perfect.

In Genesis 22:1-2, God's requested that Abraham sacrifice his son was a great test of faith. Abraham's lifelong dreams were being realized in his beloved son Isaac. Abraham believed that God had his best in mind – and Abraham was right. He believed that whatever God requested of him his obedience to God's plan was most important. His faith was in God that he would make his promises come true, even without Isaac. My faith in God's program may be confronted by similar tests.

In Leviticus 25: 1-7, the sabbatical year, was started by God as a spiritual period of rest instituted the weekly Sabbath day for the Israelites. Every seventh year was a time of rest for the land, animals and people. Their rest from work was in itself an act of faith, proving they believed God would provide for the coming year. It gave them the opportunities to reflect on the fact that God was the true provider. When I realize this truth, I am better able to commit myself into God's hands. He is more than able to provide for my needs and help me as I continue in recovery.

In Numbers 13:30, the minority report of Caleb, and later that of Joshua (14:6-9) emphasized God's power to overcome even the greatest problems. Their faith enabled them to see problems not as obstacles but as opportunities for God's power to overcome. Even the greatest problems. Their faith enabled them to see problems, not as obstacles but as opportunities for God to demonstrate his power. The basis for their faith was God's promise to restore his people from their enemies (10:9), when I have an active faith in God, my view of life and its challenges will emphasize the positive rather than the negative.

In Numbers 14:24, in contrast to the unbelief of the other Israelites, Caleb trusted God and obeyed him fully. The positive result of his faith was his entrance into the Promised Land, though he had to wait nearly forty years. The other adults, except Joshua, died as they wandered on their forty-year wilderness trek.

If I seek spiritual recovery in my own strength, I will also wander in the wilderness and never experience the wholeness God desires for me. If I step out, trusting God to lead me and protect me, I will discover a new life. Caleb and Joshua wandered in the wilderness, but through perseverance and faith in God they finally arrived.

In Numbers 21:4-9, the reference to John 3:14-15 is made evident. "And as Moses lifted up the bronze snake on a pole in the wilderness, so I the Son of Man, must be lifted up on a pole, so that everyone who believes in me will have eternal life." Evident in both passages is God's saving grace that provides salvation and healing for me who responds in faith. Healing did not come to everybody in Israel but only to those who by faith looked at the bronze snake on the pole. The apostle John makes it clear that personal forgiveness and victory over sin can come only to those who look to

Christ on the cross. In faith, God provides the powerful means of spiritual recovery from sin and failure.

In Joshua 3:7-14, God would drive out the enemies of Israel if the Israelites were obedient to him. Furthermore, so the people could see the power of God at work, the priests, acting by faith had to carry the Ark of the Covenant and stand with their feet in the Jordan River. Would God leave Joshua looking foolish, or would God act in the way he had promised? Joshua did not doubt God but had the priests stand in the river. The Jordan River was at flood stage and extremely dangerous, if not impossible to cross without God's assistance. Many times God places me where I must either stand for him or show that I don't really trust him. If I have faith in God, I can be sure he will never disappoint me.

In Joshua 6:1-14, Israel was ready to attack, but God told them to wait. God required his people to do something that on the surface seemed very foolish. They were ordered to march around the city day after day. The Israelites obeyed God and persisted in their faith, not fully understanding how God would destroy the walls of Jericho. When I experience barriers along my road to recovery, God can make those walls crumble, allowing me to be victorious. I need to do things God's way, even if I don't always understand why.

In Joshua 15:16-19, Caleb desired that not just any man marry his daughter Acsah.

He wanted a son-in-law who by faith would trust God for victory over the city of Debir. Othniel took up Caleb's challenge and defeated Debir. For his actions, Othniel received Acsah as his wife. The challenge here for my life is to place faith in God as a number one priority. So many of my problem relationships could be avoided if I trust and seek out those strong in faith rather those with prestige, power or money.

In Joshua 17:1-6, the daughter of Zelophehad demonstrated true faith in God believing that he would fulfill his promise of an inheritance to them. They based their confidence on an earlier ruling by Moses that gave them their father's inheritance because he had no sons. The faith of Zelophehad daughter was rewarded with land. God is the rewarded of faith.

In Judges 4:4-9, Deborah had served as a prophet of God in Israel. She was called to take part in a military campaign to overthrow the oppressors.   This was new ground for her and she didn't hesitate for a minute. She trusted that God would take care of her and direct her. Barak, however, put more trust in Deborah than in God. Because of his lack of trust and faith, God had to accomplish his task through another. In my own life, if I don't demonstrate the courage to lead, God decides not to use me.

In Judges 5:7, 12-15, the role of Deborah is emphasized in this song of victory. Women in ancient Israel rarely rose to positions of leadership. Deborah's courage and faith in God made her an ideal prophetess. She was called to lead the forces of Israel against the oppressive Canaanites. It took tremendous faith for Deborah to assume this unlikely position. Victory can come even when God puts me in positions where I am uncomfortable. I must have faith in God's promises to me.

In Ruth 1:16-18, Ruth's desire to remain close to Naomi was actually a step of faith. Naomi had no financial security, no family members nearby for support or protection. By staying with Naomi, Ruth was cutting herself off from her own family, land and culture. She was committing her life into God's hands. Ruth stood by Naomi, doing all she could to provide food and help her mother-in-law. The process of spiritual recovery is not an easy road. I must realize this as I commit my life to it. Sticking to this commitment will always yield great rewards in the long run.

In Samuel 1:9-11, Hannah breathed a beautiful prayer through her tears. In Faith, she not only committed her infertility to God, but to surrender to God's service the son he might give to her. I must realize that without God's intervention, I am helpless to overcome any of the problems or dependencies. I might have. Learning to give up control and completely rely on God is a step I need to take.

In 1 Kings 17:8-16, the widow of Zarephath demonstrated the delivering power of faith. She and her son faced starvation, but still shared the last of her food with Elijah. She believed that God would come through. So she gave up her last resources for survival. The result was her deliverance. God provided for her needs. When I am powerless – at the end of my rope –all I need to do is call out to God. God will take care of and deliver me from my dependence if I am willing to trust him.

.

In 2 Kings 6:14-20, Elisha's servant was terrified by the awesome Aramean army because he couldn't see the help available to him. He was unaware of the great army of heavenly soldiers on his side. As I face the difficult task of spiritual recovery and physical challenges, I am tempted to give up. But as I begin to see through the eyes of faith, I discover the awesome power available to me. God's power is far greater than enemy I might face. When I admit my powerlessness and place my faith in God for help, I will find his power more than sufficient for my needs.

In Chronicles 2:42-55, God rewards faith. These verses are devoted to the family of Caleb, one of the twelve spies Moses sent into Canaan. Caleb, along with Joshua, brought back a positive report based entirely upon his faith in God's provision. Caleb refused to be discouraged by difficult obstacles. He believed that God could overcome anything he might face. My challenges should not stop me in my spiritual recovery process. Like Caleb, I should remember that God is able to overcome anything I might face. God is my source of true victory.

In 1 Chronicles 4:9-10, Jabez is another example of faith. In the midst of his difficulties, and in spite of his name, his name means "distress" or "pain". Jabez looked to God for the solution to his problems. He prayed that God would keep him from fulfilling the meaning of his name. I found this prayer worthwhile. I don't cause pain to others; instead I should try to be a blessing to them.

In 1 Chronicles 14:16-17, David did as God commanded and God granted him success. Simple obedience and faith was the key to David's victory. I know that if I have enough faith or if I follow certain instructions, I may not experience an immediate cure. My obedience and faith may bring new and difficult circumstances. As I go through difficult times, I need not fear that God has rejected me. He uses these situations to work his will in me. God will always stand with me, even if he doesn't give me an immediate cure.

In 2 Chronicles 13:1-9, Abijah was about to go into battle where his army was vastly outnumbered. Instead of giving into fear, he stood firm because of his faith in God's promises. As I grow in God's word, I will battle many difficult situations. When I try to face them alone, I will fail. I need to stand on the many promises God has given me in Scripture and trust him to deliver me. I need to live by faith when it is impossible to live by sight.

In 2 Chronicles 32: 3-6, I have faith in God – and work hard to do his will. Hezekiah gives me an excellent example of how I should act in my spiritual recovery – with both faith and hard work. He knows that only God could deliver Judah from the Assyrian invasion, but that did not stop him from doing what he could to protect Jerusalem. One of the engineering marvels of the ancient world is Hezekiah's tunnel that brought water into the city from a spring outside the city walls. The tunnel ensured a steady water supply during a siege. Hezekiah had faith in God for victory, but he made certain that he did all he could do to prepare for the invasion.

In Proverbs 16:33, there is no such thing as luck. Everything that happens to me, even the seemingly random call of the dice, is under the watchful eye and guiding hand of God. It is a challenge to my faith to trust that God is truly in control and that he cares about all the details of my life. It is joyful to remember that "God causes everything to work together for the good of those who love God and are called according to his purpose for the." (Romans 8:28)

In Jeremiah 26:12-15, because of Jeremiah's faith, he was able to speak boldly for God, even when his life was threatened. Sometimes, I, like Peter, deny that I know God when I face opposition. It is easy for me to claim to have faith when everything is going well. The depth of my faith, however, is measured when I am under pressure. I should never let others' opinions keep me from sharing what I know about God and his powers to deliver me from bondage.

In Daniel 3: 3-15, Shadrach, Meshach and Abednego displayed great faith and courage when they refused to bow to the statute. Nebuchadnezzar confronted them and issued an ultimatum. Either bow down or die in a blazing furnace. He reminds me of people who tried to bully their way through life, abusing others who won't give in to their pressure. These people, however, are no match for God. He will standby me, protecting me from the various abusive personalities I encounter. .

In Habakkuk, 3:17-19, With Habakkuk's

prayer, came a climax in a beautiful affirmation of faith. Even though there would be difficult times ahead, Habakkuk knew that he could trust God to provide for him. With the strength he needed to persevere, this verse provides a surefooted confidence I can have in my God. He is my strength and safety.

In Zechariah 2:8-10, for the spiritual recovery exiles, the test of faith was simple — love for others, especially the helpless widows, orphans, foreigners, and the poor. The ultimate proof of my willingness to help others is the final proof of my spiritual recovery. As I reach out to others to offer them the second chance that I have already received, I will discover the joy of loving others and my own spiritual recovery will be heard as a result.

Chapter 5

Obedience

In the following passages I want to explore Obedience. I look at obedience as love and as my spiritual mirror. It's like looking into the mirror and washing my face. If I see something wrong, I can take the proper steps to fix it.

James uses a similar illustration to show God's love should be like a spiritual mirror in my life. He said, "And remembers it's a message to obey and love, not just to listen to. If you don't obey, you are only fooling yourself. For if you just listen and don't obey, it is like looking at your face in a mirror but do nothing to improve your appearance. You see yourself, walk away, and forget what you look like. But if you keep looking steadily into God's perfect law – the law that sets you free – and if you do what it says and don't forget what you heard, then God will bless you for doing it." (James 1:22-25). As I examine my life, I need to respond with immediate action if something has changed since I last looked. I need to correct problems promptly.

In Matthew 4:8-10, Jesus was tempted by the devil. He didn't fall for this trick and remained obedient in love to his Father.

I need to beware of "shortcuts" that take me even one step outside of God's will. In James 4:7, Resist the Devil, and he will flee from you." There are no quick fixes in life. The path to spiritual recovery may be long and hard, but by obeying God and staying on the path, I will find the good things in life has for me,

In Psalm 111:10, the psalmist wrote, "Reverence for the Lord", is the foundation of true wisdom. The rewards of wisdom come to all that obey him" God has clearly given me instructions as the basis for all my decisions.

In Matthew 7:24-25, Jesus said, "Anyone who listens to my teachings and obeys me is wise, like a person who builds a house on solid rock. Though the rains come in torrents and the floodwaters rise and the winds beat against that house, it won't collapse, because it is built on rock. "Listening to what the Bible says is the next step toward walking in wisdom and honesty. By filling my mind with God's instructions, they will help me to follow them. The book of Job (Job 28:28), tells me, "the fears of the

Lord is true wisdom; to forsake evil is real understanding."

Turning my life over, surrendering my will, obeying this word, sounds like a good move for me. These elements are necessary - reverence for God, listening to His instructions, and following them.

In the book of Joshua, God gave the Israelites instructions for every area of their lives. Joshua was obedient. The people, however, waivered and were inconsistent. This brought them trouble. What was true is Joshua's day is still true for me. The more I trust and believe God, the more I want to obey Him. The more I obey Him, the greater my joy, regardless of my circumstances. My obedience to God is something not to be resisted. Obedience is the only pathway to a life filled with joy and love.

In 1 Samuel, I'm again confronted with the importance of obedience as love since I want to recover from my abuse issues and face my physical challenges. To God, "obedience is far better than sacrifice." (1 Samuel:22). In Saul's case, his lack of obedience led to his downfall. David, on the other hand, was a man after God's own heart. He trusted and obeyed God. Even when he could have killed Saul, he refused because Saul was God's anointed King. And even though David failed and sinned, he repented and turned back to God. I need to be encouraged by Saul's actions. I realize I cannot live a flawless life. I need to trust

God and do my best to love and obey him.

Eli, Samuel and David felt the consequences of disobedience when they disobeyed God. Their sin affected not only themselves but also their children. Saul's disobedience destroyed not only himself, but also the majority of his family. Saul had various opportunities to get his life back on track, but his self-centered heart blocked him from looking to God for helping and healing. Saul's lack of faith and obedience resulted in a bitter life and tragic death.

2 Chronicles 1 was written to encourage the Jews after their return from Babylonian exile. The people hit bottom during the humiliating captivity. When they returned to rebuild their temple, land and nation,

God wanted them to remember and learn that any successful rebuilding program centers on love and obedience and true worship of God.

I need to remember the lesson. The Israelites struggled to grasp throughout their history. My life begins, survives and continues through complete dependence upon God.

This book also emphasizes the necessity of faithfulness and obedience. When a King came along who was faithful and obedient to God, the people experienced spiritual recovery and restoration. Today, there was victory, tomorrow trials. I need to preserve in my faithfulness and obedience through each new day. I need to incorporate the principles learned in my daily life.

Through obedience there is always hope. Even when my life seems bleakest, God is at work. When I am overwhelmed by circumstances and feel that God has forgotten me, it might be helpful for me to remember that I am feeling what the people of Judah must have felt in Babylon – that all is lost. In the midst of their despair, King Cyprus of Persia sent out a proclamation that allowed God's people to return to Jerusalem to rebuild their Temple. When I surrender and turn my life over to God, I can be confident even in my darkest hours, God is at work. There is hope.

In Jeremiah 1, obedience and faithfulness overcomes failure. From my human perspective, Jeremiah was a failure to God. Jeremiah was one of the greatest successes in the Bible. Jeremiah remained faithful to God and his commandments despite powerful opposition. Sometimes I feel my obstacles are too big to overcome and my weaknesses too much of a liability. When I feel discouraged, I need to remember that God simply wants me to be obedient and faithful – to keep going. I don't have to be a raving success. I just need to be faithful in the long haul. God will honor my faithfulness by providing me the strength I need for the next step.

Jeremiah has been called the weeping prophet, he did more than cry – he was bitter, angry, discouraged, depressed and lonely. I have experienced these feelings.

Jeremiah even complained to God (15:17-18). "I sat alone because your hand was on me…..Your help seems as uncertain as a seasonal brook. It is like a spring that has gone dry." How often I feel this way. God's acceptance of Jeremiah's emotions shows me that I am free to bring all of my failures and strong feelings to God. He accepts and understands me just as I am, and is ready to heal my brokenness and pain if I am honest with him.

Jeremiah told the people about the "new covenant" that God had for them. (31:1-40. God loved them and had a wonderful future planned for them, despite their impending doom. The Lord told them, "For I know the plans I have for you. They are plans for good and not for disaster, to give you a future and a hope." (29:11)

In Ames 1, God honors those whose hearts are upright and obedient. Many of the people of Israel carried on the outward appearance of religion even though they abandoned their faith in God. God wants me to be obedient and possess a genuine heart that seeks to know him better and trust him more. God cares about the attitudes of my heart.

The letter to the Ephesians is my favorite book in the Bible. This letter reminds me that when I trust and obey God as my Savior, he adopts me into a new family. In this family, God is my perfect and loving father. God, my father, is perfect and becoming a part of His family is an all-important step in my spiritual recovery and facing physical challenges. I'm still estranged from my old family.

In the book of Ephesians, Jesus Christ is exalted as the focus of all history and as the only means of experiencing a meaningful life. The letter urges me to keep Christ at the center of all I do, maintaining conscious contact and obedience with Him daily.

In 1 Timothy, Paul shows the importance of obedience and love in discipline. Obedience and discipline go hand in hand to develop a strong spiritual recovery program and face my physical challenges. I need to stay in good spiritual and emotional condition in order to receive the powerful help that God offers me. I must be obedient and disciplined and continue to take personal inventory and right the wrongs. I need to be involved with activities that increase my conscious contact with God.

More underling themes of obedience appear in 1 Timothy when Paul urged Timothy to preserve the Christian faith and speak only the truth. Timothy opposed false teachers who were trying to undermine his work. Paul's only weapons were the truth about Christ and a godly lifestyle. Through obedience, I am able to defend and share the message of God's healing powers through belief in Christ. Paul knew that only the truth about God in Jesus Christ could bring healing and recovery to broken people. Jesus offers me true freedom. My job is to defend and share the message of God's healing power through belief in Christ. I can accomplish this by speaking the truth about God's power and backing up my words with my transformed life.

Obedience is hope and love. Paul's advice on how to relate to the people in his church is important in my relationships as well. Especially, as I carry the message of hope to others. By caring for each other, I am demonstrating God's power at work within me.

The importance of obedience and faithfulness, as opposition mounts as I pursue recovery, I must stay on track and be obedient. Opposition enters my life when important changes are taking place.

Actually, I feel most people want to change. My job is to remain obedient and faithful to my spiritual growth. Paul was faithful to God, and he called Timothy to follow his example. God calls each of us to do the same.

The power of God's word is evident when Paul challenged Timothy to know and obey God's instructions (2:15). Paul described how God's message helps me as it teaches me what is true, and allows me to see what is wrong in my life. It points me in the right direction and helps me do what is right. (3:15) Praying and thinking focuses me on God's word for it equips me to live as God wants me to live.

In Genesis, one has to wonder whether

God's instructions made any sense to Noah. God told him to build a gigantic boat far from the nearest body of navigable water. Noah was obedient even though God's instructions were hard to understand. I may not understand how everything works, but to do what God tells me is necessary for spiritual growth. When I step out in faith, as Noah did, God will give me the success I seek.

Noah listens to God and obeyed His requests. The Ark was floating over the earth on the floodwaters – not an ideal situation to be in. God didn't forget about Noah. It's comforting to know that when I obey God, he will not forget me. He will stand by me until his plans for me are complete.

In Genesis 22:1-2, God's request that Abraham sacrifice his son was a great test of faith and obedience. Abraham's lifelong dreams were being realized in his beloved son Isaac. Abraham believed that God had his best in mind – and Abraham was right. No matter what God required of him, his obedience to God's plan was most important. He trusted that God would make his promises come true, even without Isaac. My faith in God's program may be confronted by similar tests.

In Leviticus 8:30-36, Aaron and his sons were sprinkled with blood from the sacrifices. This symbolized their cleansing and reconciliation to God through the sacrificial death of the animal offering. The high price of their sin, the death of a living animal, would have been a poignant reminder of how important obedience was held. Because of the high price paid for my sins, the sacrificial death of Christ on the cross, I need to be living a life of obedience to his word.

In Numbers 15:37-41, the Israelites were required to wear tassels on the corners of their clothing. This reminded them constantly of their covenant relationship with God and the need to obey Him. It was a visual reminder that their commitment to obey God was important in every realm of life. This ritual doesn't exist today, but its principals are helpful. As I commit my life to God, I need to realize that obedience to Him is important in all areas of life.

In Deuteronomy 7, 6:18, one of the biblical formulas for success state "Do what is right and good in the Lord's sight, so all will go well with you." Sounds simple? Hardly. God laid out a plan for successful and healthy living in the Israelite community. Most of these laws and principles apply to me as well. God gave me instructions for living a healthy, joy filled life. He desires the best for me. This encourages me to seek to follow his program, as difficult as that may be. I knew that when God's instructions become too difficult for me, he is right there to help me.

In Deuteronomy 10, 12-13, God's pattern for godly living begins with a proper respect for him ("fear him) and a healthy lifestyle ("live according to his will"). By truly loving God and living his way, obedience to him is a natural response ("obey the Lord's commands and laws"). This book teaches me that God's laws are given to me for my own good. If my obedience is pure, I should have healthy attitudes and love for God ("love and worship Him"). God's pattern for living is in my best interest, and it would be wise for me to follow it.

In Deuteronomy 11, obedience to God's instructions should be a direct result of my love for Him. My love for God is the major motivating force in my obedience to the civil, ceremonial and moral obligations he requests of me. My love and obedience should be a natural response to the love he has shown to me.

In Deuteronomy 15, 16-18, the servant who serves out of necessity and then out of devotion is similar to the way I relate to God, my Savior and me. As I mature in my walk with God, my obedience grows out of my love for Him. I soon realize (though difficult) that everything that God requires of me is for my own good.

In Deuteronomy 28:1-6, these verses reveal the one essential requirement for God's blessings – obedience. I am to obey and love God and respond to his commandments. As a result, there are blessings for me. In recovery and facing physical challenges, I seek to know God's will for me and then proceed to do it.

In Joshua 6:1-14, Israel was ready to

attack, but God told them to wait. On the surface, this seems foolish. God commanded them to march around the city day after day. The Israelites obeyed God and persisted in their faith, not fully understanding how God would destroy the walls of Jericho. When I hit seemingly unbreakable barriers along the road to recovery, God makes those barriers crumble down, allowing me to be victorious. But, I need to do things his way, even if I don't always understand why.

In 1 Samuel 2, 1-3, note Hannah's prayer of rejoicing, "My heart rejoices in the Lord! Oh, how the Lord has blessed me!" She praised the one responsible for her deliverance – God himself. God delivered her from the trauma of infertility and gave her a son. Obedience was surely difficult, even painful as it might be at times, and will ultimately bring me joy. It also brings blessings to the people close to me.

In 1 Chronicles 28:8-11, David took the time to pass God's wisdom on to Solomon. He started to acknowledge God's promise of a dynasty that would rule Israel forever. David recognized that in order to receive the blessings of this great promise, Solomon and his descendants were responsible to obey God's commands. Obedience and love to God's will is the only pathway to blessing me.

In 2 Chronicles 14: 1-2, we learn that the world's measure of success is not the same as God's measure. Every action, attitude, decision and feelings needs to be measured by the criteria suggested by Asa's life. "Asa and what was pleasing and good is the sight of the Lord his God." Obedience to the revealed will of God is a vital step in the rebuilding process – my life.

In Psalm 119:9-16, obedience to God's word produces wholeness. It is only logical that I should do all I can to follow it. Through Scriptures, God has left clear guidelines for how he expects me to live. He has promised that he will help me carry out his will if I sincerely ask him. By studying and applying God's message, my life will become a joyful experience that will implant God's truth finally in my mind and heart.

In Ecclesiastes 7, it states that God is in control of the world. He created the world and the laws that govern it. Following this plan makes sense. Doing things God's way will lead to harmony with God, with other people and the world we live in. I will never understand everything about my world or why things happen the way they do some things in my life don't make any sense, but God is in control. By trusting him and obeying his plan for healthy living, I can live a productive and joyful life.

In Jeremiah, 5:21-22, a proper reverence for God and his awesome power inspires me to trust God and obey him. This attitude protects me from the dependence and problems that could devour me. Reverence for God leads to faith, obedience, honesty and love - all-important aspects of a solid spiritual program.

In Jeremiah 7:8-11, many of God's people believed that God's presence in the Temple would protect them from enemy attack, regardless of whether or not they obeyed God's laws. But the people of Judah were not excused from obedience and neither am I. I am not the exception to the rule. God controls this world, and his plan for healthy living in his message is the only program worth following.

In Jeremiah 41, 1-12, we see for the first time since Jeremiah's prophetic work began peace and harmony in the lives of God's people. They were following God's directive to serve Nebuchadnezzar. They were obeying God. There is peace within me when I seek to follow God's will for me,

In Micah 4:1-5, if everyone loved and obeyed God, this world would be filled with peace, harmony and prosperity. Life would be meaningful and joyful. God desires that I live in a world of joy and harmony. If I admit my failures and seek to live according to his will for me, there is still hope that my corner of the world can reflect God's good intentions for wellness and peace.

In Matthew 21: 28-32, I'm reminded of addictive years when I was like the first son, saying no to his father's wishes. I turned my back to God and indulged in selfish desires. I changed, however, when I saw where I was headed. My change of heart and lifestyle will gain me eternal life.

In Luke 5:4-11, the disciples were definitely persistent in their fishing, but doing things their way just wasn't enough. As soon as they followed Jesus' advice, they experienced success. I cannot attain spiritual recovery or face my physical challenges alone. But if I'm not doing things God's way, no amount of hard work will bring success. Following God's will for my life will lead me to healing and success. As I follow God's program obediently and seek his gracious help, I will experience his powerful deliverance.

In John 21:1-14, John speaks about the disciples and their fishing. When Jesus said to them to throw the net on the other side of the boat, the disciple's first response was maybe laugh. By obeying Jesus, they caught so many fish the net began to break. I cannot do it alone. I need to follow God's instructions for healthy living. As I trust God and obey his will, I learn that God's power can build my life.

In Ephesians 4:31-32, a life of spiritual recovery committed to knowing God better through prayer and meditation on his word. In looking at my life, I realize just how demanding God's standard for righteous living are. God's grace helps me conform to his will and I need not despair. As I obey Him, he will teach me to live without bitterness, anger or harsh words. God wants to heal my relationships. When I do things his way, I am well on the way to reconciling with alienated friends and building solid foundations for my spiritual growth.

In Philippians 2:12-18, Paul writes that obedience to God's program is one of the requirements for spiritual growth. God not only wants me to live a godly life, he wants to provide me with the power to do it. He works in me, giving me the desire and the ability to obey Him. As I get to know God by reading the Bible and spending time with Him in prayer, he can transform me from the inside out so I can shine brightly for Him.

In Titus 2:11-15, Paul writes that when we realize how much God loves me and provides the power for me to live a godly life, I am motivated to entrust my life to Him and seek his will. The proper response to God's grace is right conduct. When I obey God, he loves me and desires to help me succeed. I don't need to fear God because of my sins. He still loves me and will help me rebuild my life when I admit my failures to Him. This can give me hope as I work through spiritual recovery and physical challenges and attain spiritual awareness.

Chapter 6

The 12 Step Path

I mentioned earlier that I am a recovering alcoholic and found the twelve steps of Alcoholic Anonymous the path to spiritual recovery. Also, I have found the Bible a one-step spiritual program that enriches my spiritual growth.

Genesis 16:1-15 - Step 1

In Step One, I admitted I am powerless over my alcoholism and physical challenges – that my life had become unmanageable.

Sometimes I am powerless because of my situation in life. I may be in a situation where other people have power over me. I may feel trapped by the demands of others and that there's no way to plan them all. Sometimes I feel stuck and frustrated with my relationships or physical challenges. I used to look for a measure of control by escaping through my behavior.

Hagan is a picture of powerlessness. She had no rights. As a girl, she was a slave to Sarai and Abram. When they were upset because Sarai could not have children, Hagan was given to Abram as a surrogate. When she became pregnant, as they wished, Sarai was so jealous that she beat Hagan, and Hagan ran away. In the wilderness all alone, Hagan was met by an angel who gave her an amazing message, "Return to your mistakes and submit to her authority.' The angel added, 'I will give you more descendants than you can count,' And the angel also said, 'you are now pregnant and will give birth to a son. You are to name him Ishmael, for the Lord has heard about your misery.'" (Genesis 16:9-11),

Sometimes it's tempting to run away through escape hatches. When this happens, God is there and he is listening to my woes. I hope to express my pain to God instead of just trying to escape it. He hears me cry and is there to give me hope for the future.

Judges 16:1-31 - Step 1

When I refused to admit my powerlessness, I am only deceiving myself. The lies I used to tell myself and others were inching me closer to disorderly life.

Samson was one of Israel's judges. As a

child, he had been dedicated to God and gifted him with supernatural strength. Samson, however, had a lifelong weakness - women. Delilah blinded him to the dangers he faced with her. Samson's enemies were paying her to discover the secret of his strength. Samson finally revealed his secret, was taken captive and died a slave.

Samson's real problem can be found in the lies he told himself. By not admitting his powerlessness, he remained blind to the obvious danger that his pride and desire for beautiful women were leading him. I need to be careful not to fall into a similar trap. As I learn to acknowledge my powerlessness over my alcoholism and physical challenges, I will become more aware of behaviors that will likely lead me to destruction.

2 Kings 5:1-15   Step 1

I have many times felt humiliated to admit that I am powerless, especially if I am used to being in control. I am powerful over my actions, efforts and attitudes, but out of control in terms of my addiction and physical challenges. When I refused to admit my powerlessness, I lost everything. Those unmanageable parts of my life may infect and destroy everything else.

The experience of Aramean army commander Naaman, illustrate how this is true. He had leprosy and lost everything.

Naaman heard about a prophet in Israel who could heal him. He found the prophet, and the prophet told him that in order to be healed he needed to dip himself seven times in the Jordan River. His power couldn't buy him an instant and easy cure. In the end, however, he acknowledged his powerlessness, followed the instructions and recovered completely.

My challenges are as life threatening as the leprosy of Naaman's day. There is no instant or easy cure. The only answer is to admit my powerless, humble myself and submit to the process that will eventually bring healing.

Job 6:2-13   Step 1

Sometimes I felt so confused and overwhelmed by the pain in my life that everything seemed hopeless. No matter what I did, I was powerless to change things for the better. The weight of pain and sadness seemed too heavy to bear.

Job felt that way. He'd lost everything, even though he had always done what was right. His ten children were dead. Job had lost his business, his riches and his health.

Job didn't know that the end of his life would be even better than the beginning. God eventually restored everything Job had lost and then some. He died an old man having lived a long life.

Even when I'm pressed to the point of desperation, there is still hope that my life will change. My spiritual walk could be so complete that the final lines written could say, "As Martin he died, after living a long, good life." I need to remember that life can be good again.

Mark 10:13-16 Step 1

For me in recovery, memories of my childhood are full of the terrors with being powerless. We never had family functions. We had family dysfunctions. I made a vow never to be as vulnerable as I was when I was a child.

Jesus tells me that in order to enter the Kingdom of Heaven, I must become a precious child, and this involves being powerless. He said, "I assure you, anyone who doesn't have this kind of faith will never get into the Kingdom of Heaven of

God." (Mark 10:15)

Precious children are singularly reliant on the love, care and nurture of others for their basic needs. They must trust their lives to someone who is more powerful than they, and hopefully, they will be heard and lovingly cared for.

I, too, must admit that I am truly powerless if my life is to become healthy. This doesn't mean that I have to become a victim again. Admitting my powerlessness is an honest appraisal of my situation in life and a positive step in my spiritual walk.

Acts: 9: 1-9   Step 1

There are important events in my life

that changed my destiny. These events are times when I'm confronted with how powerless I am over them. I decided that these moments forever set the course of my life in a much better direction.

Saul of Tarsus (later called Paul) had his moment. After Jesus' ascension, Saul took it upon himself to rid the world of Christians. As he headed for Damascus on this mission, A bright light from heaven blinded Saul. He was blinded for three days.

Saul was confronted with the fact that his life was not as perfect as he thought. Self-righteousness was his trademark. When he let go his illusions of power, he became one of the most powerful men ever—the apostle Paul. I'm confronted with the knowledge that my life isn't under control. But, I do have a choice. I can continue in denial or I can face the fact that I have been blind to some important issues. In my walk, I have been shown a new way of life. My deafness is my blessing from God.

2 Corinthians 4:7-10   Step 1

By admitting my powerless, I won't be tempted to give up completely in the struggle against physical challenges and addiction. I know it doesn't make sense that I admit powerlessness and still find the strength to go on. This irony will be dealt in

Step 2 and 3.

Life is full of paradoxes. The apostle

tells me in 2 Corinthians 4:7-8, "this precious treasure – this light and power that now within me – is held in delicate containers, that is, in our weak bodies. So everyone can see that our glorious power is from God and is not our own. We are pressed on every side by troubles, but we are not crushed and broken."

The picture here contrasts a precious treasure. The living power of God pours into my life from spirit. My human body, with all the flaws and weaknesses, is my perishable container. As a human being, I am perfectly human.

I don't have to be strong or pretend to be perfect. I am learning to live my life with its daily struggles, in a human body inundated with weaknesses and still find the power from above to keep going without being crushed and broken.

Daniel 4:19-33   Step 2

When I was caught up in my alcoholism, it was for me to deny the truth about my situation with grandiose thinking. I thought I was above it all, accountable to none.

In his day, Nebuchadnezzar, King of ancient Babylon, was the most powerful ruler on earth. He believed he was a god and demanded to be worshipped. Through Daniel, God said to him, "This is…what the Most High has declared will happen to you. You will be driven from human society, and you will live in the fields with the wild animals…until you learn that the Most High rules over the Kingdom of the world and gives them to anyone he chooses." (Daniel 14:24-25)

This happened just as Daniel predicted. At the end of the King's time in exile, he said, "I…looked up to heaven. My sanity returned to me, so did my honor and glory and Kingdom," (Daniel 4:34, 36-37)

I am not God. I am accountable to God. God can remedy my "insanity". God will do so if I entrust my life to Him.

Mark 5: 1-13   Step 2

When I gave up on my physical

challenges and alcoholism, I let go of an uncanny force. (The Devil). Before then, I almost gave up on me because I stopped trying. Whether this behavior was self-induced or whatever, God is available to restore me to sanity and wholeness.

Jesus helped a man who was acting insanely. In Mark 5:3-5. "This man lived among the tombs and could not be restrained, even with a chain. Whenever he was put into chains and shackle – as he often was – he snapped the chains from his wrists and smashed the shackles. No one was strong enough to control him. All day long and throughout the night, he would wander among the tombs and in the hills, screaming and hitting himself with stone." Jesus went into the graveyard and dealt with the forces of darkness that were afflicting the man and restore him to sanity. I struggled to be free from the control of society and loved ones, only to discover that my bondage doesn't come from outside sources. All hope seems lost, but where there is still life, there is hope. God can touch my craziness and restore me to sanity.

Luke 8:43-48   Step 2

Faith is a key to successfully working my spiritual journey. I nearly exhausted all of my own resources trying to overcome my physical challenges before I risked believing in God.

While Jesus lived on earth, He was known for his healing powers that crowds of sick people constantly pressed in on him. In Luke 8:43-44, 34, "there was a woman in the crowd who had had a hemorrhage for twelve years. She had spent everything on doctors and still could find no cure. She came up behind Jesus and touched Him, because she felt healing power go out from Him. Immediately, the bleeding stopped". Jesus said to her, "Your faith has made you well. Go in peace."

I cannot afford to stand back hoping for cures, and avoid deliberate action because of my lack of faith. I came to believe in Jesus, my Lord and Savior, and to take a stand with faith in my spiritual walk.

Luke 15:11-24   Step 2

One day I woke up and realized that my physical challenges and alcoholism were overcoming me. I lived like an animal in terms of my physical surroundings.

A young man took an early inheritance and traveled away from home. When his money was spent, the women just a memory, and the magic high long gone, he resorted to slopping pigs to earn a meager living. He became so hungry he eyed the pigs slop with envy, and realized he had a problem. "When he finally came to his senses, he said to himself, 'At home even the hired men have food enough to spare, and here I am, dying of hunger! I will go home to my father....'so he returned home to his father. And while he was still a long distance away, his father saw him coming.

Filled with love and compassion, he ran to his son, embraced him, and kissed him," (Luke 15:17-18, 20)

There is hope for a better way of life. I am reminded of times when life was good, and I long to have that goodness restored. As I turn to God, who is powerful to help me build something better, I will turn to God, I will discover that His power can restore me to sanity.

Romans 1:18-20   Step 2

Saying that I came to trust, suggests a process. Forming beliefs and trusting of what it means to be made in God's image, it involves emotion and logic that leads to action.

Looking back at my own experiences, I see what doesn't work. Looking at the condition of my life, I realize that I don't have enough power alone to conquer my physical challenges. I tried with all my might, but to no avail. When I quiet my mind enough to listen, I hear that still, small voice inside saying, "There is a God and He is extremely powerful." Paul said it this way in Romans 1:19, "For the truth about God is known to all people instinctively. God has put this knowledge in their hearts."

Recognizing my internal weaknesses is the first step in my spiritual walk. When I look beyond myself, I see others who have struggled with physical challenges and addictions and yet recovered; I know in my heart that God helped them. And God will help me.

Hebrews 11:1-10   Step 2

"What is faith?" the Bible asks. In Hebrews 11:1, "It is the confident assurance that what we hope for is going to happen. It is evidence of things we cannot see."

The Bible teaches me that the key is in the nature of God. In Hebrews, 11:6, I am told, "anyone who wants to come to Him must believe that there is a God as one who is reaching out to help me, I become more anxious to look for Him. I start each day by asking God to help me have more faith. I then ask Him for the courage and strength to hope and plan for a better future.

Deuteronomy 30:15-20 Step 3

Jesus tells me that he did not trust the men around him because he knew what was in their hearts. Jesus, however, voluntarily turned his life over to the will of God the Father. "It is better to trust the Lord than to put confidence in people". (Psalm 118:8).

I have learned in the past that putting confidence in people brings pain and disappointment. I can't let this keep me from ever believing or trusting again.

In Numbers 23:19, "God is not a man that he should lie, and He is not a human, that he should change his mind". In Hebrews 13:5, God said, "I will never fail you. I will never forsake you." I know that I can't make it all alone. Today, I turn my life over to God who is really able to care for my needs.

Deuteronomy 30:15-20   Step 3

I have been given the choice to choose – This freedom of choice brings with it the burden of the consequences of my choices. These choices affect my life. Free will is my blessing and my responsibility. In Deuteronomy 30:15-20, "Choose to love the Lord your God and to obey Him and commit yourself to Him, for He is your life". I can choose to set my heart in the direction of life

Psalm 61:1-8   Step 3

Turning my life and will over to God can be attractive and rewarding. When I give in to my physical challenges and dependences, I am giving control over to the Devil. In other words, I gave up personal responsibility for my life.

There are certain steps, I can take to change my focus and turn my life over to God. In Ephesians 5:18, Paul comments, "don't be drunk with wine, because that will ruin your life. Instead, let the Holy Spirit fill and control you."

When I'm overwhelmed and in need of some kind of escape, I have a new place to turn. In Psalm 9:9-10, King David says, "The Lord is a shelter for the oppressed, a refuge in times of troubles. Those who know your name trust in you, for you, O Lord, have never abandoned anyone who searches for you."

In Psalm 61:2-3, David also wrote, "From the ends of the earth, I will cry to you for help, for my heart is overwhelmed. Lead I to the towering rock of safety, for you are my safe refuge, a fortress where my enemies cannot reach me."

Genesis 3:6-13   Step 4

My earlier life was spent in a state of hiding and I was ashamed of who I was inside. Step 4 involved uncovering the things I have been hiding, even from myself.

After Adam and Eve disobeyed God, "they suddenly felt shame at their nakedness. So they strung fig leaves together around their hips to cover themselves…the Lord called to Adam, 'Where are you? He replied, 'I heard you, so I hid. I was afraid because I was naked.'" (Genesis 3:7-10).

When the real person inside me came out of hiding, I needed to deal with him. I uncovered the hidden parts of myself that will enable me to change the outer person.

Nehemiah 8:7-10   Step 4

I know that the bottom line is that there

is an enormous amount of sadness awaiting me, and I fear the pain that facing the grief will bring.

"Don't weep on such a day as this! For today is a sacred day before the Lord your God.... Go and celebrate with a feast of choice foods and sweet drinks, and, share gifts of food with people who have nothing prepared...Don't be dejected and sad, for the joy of the Lord is your strength!"

When I get out to face the pain and sadness at making a spiritual inventory, I need the "joy of the Lord", to give me strength. This joy comes from recognizing even celebrating God's ability to bring me out of bondage and care for me as I pass through the sadness toward a new way of life.

2 Corinthians 7:8-11   Step 4

I know I have to deal with sorrow. I tried to stuff it down and ignore it. But sorrow doesn't go away. I need to accept the sorrow that will be part of my spiritual inventory,

In 2 Corinthians 7:9-11, Paul writes, "Now I am glad I sent it, not because it hurt you, but because the pain caused you to have remorse and change your ways...For God can use sorrow in our lives to help us turn away from sin and seek salvation.

The Corinthians' grief was good – it came from honest self-evaluation, not morbid self-condemnation. I can learn to accept my sorrow as a positive part of my spiritual walk, not as a punishment.

Hosea 11:8-11   Step 5

I'm aware of the deep shame, troubles and pain I caused my family because of my physical challenges and alcoholism. I was afraid to admit my sins because I didn't believe God could love me.

Hosea was a prophet to the rebellious nation of Israel. God used Hosea's life to demonstrate his unconditional love for his people and me. God told Hosea to marry a prostitute. He married her, loved her and devoted himself to her. She relapsed into her old ways and broke Hosea's heart. God baffled Hosea by telling him, "Go and get your wife again. Bring her back to you and love her, even though she loves adultery. For the Lord still loves Israel even though the people have turned to other gods." (Hosea 3:1)

How can God still love me…In Hosea 11:8-9, "Oh, how can I give you up…? How can I let you go? How can I destroy you…? My heart is torn within me, and my compassion overflows…."

There is nothing I can do or confess to God that would cause him to stop loving me.

Amos 7:7-8

The prophet Amos recorded this vision

Martin J. McNamara

in Amos 7:7-8, "I saw the Lord standing beside a wall that had been built using a plumb line. He was checking it with a plumb line to see if was straight. And the Lord said, 'I will test my people with this plumb line.'"

A plumb line is a device used to measure the straightness of a wall to see just how Israel measured up to his righteous standards. The same rule holds true in the spiritual realm. God's word is my spiritual plumb line. I can't argue with the spiritual laws revealed in the Bible. I measure my life by the plumb line of God's word. When things don't add up, I need to admit there is a problem and start rebuilding.

Genesis 23:1-4   Step 6

210

The pathway to spiritual recovery involves the death process. Giving up my past and sins is often like suffering the death of a loved one.

Abraham and his grandson Jacob both lost loved ones as they traveled to the Promised Land. In Genesis 23:1-4, 19, "Sarah…died at Kiriatha-arba (now called Hebron) in the land of Canaan. There Abraham mourned and wept for her. Then, leaving her body, he said, 'Here I am, a stranger in a foreign land, with no place to bury my wife. Please let me have a piece of land for a burial plot'…"

As I continue my journey in my new life, I will necessarily lose some of my old ways of coping. I need to stop and take time to give my losses a proper burial. I must put them away, cover the shame, and allow myself to grieve the loss of something very close to me. When my time of grieving is over, I too, can journey on.

Psalm 51:16-19   Step 6

If I have honestly worked the previous steps and repented for my sins, I know I have found enough pain inside myself to break my heart. Looking at my brokenness is part of the human condition that is crushing. This represents a sign from God that I am ready for him to change me.

John 5:1-15   Step 6

I know I am honestly ready for God to

remove my past sins. I know I cannot work them perfectly. My part is to keep moving to get close as I can to being ready.

In John 5:5-9, John writes about a pool where people went hoping for a miraculous healing. There was a man who went there who had been sick for thirty-eight years. He told Jesus that no one was there to help him into the pool. Jesus healed this crippled man.

This man was so crippled he couldn't go any farther on his own. He camped as near as he could to a place where there was hope for recovery. God met him there and brought him the rest of the way. For me, "entirely ready" may mean getting as close to the hope of healing as I can in my own crippled condition. God meets me there and takes me the rest of the way..

Isaiah 57:12-19   Step 7

Step 7 forms a bridge between the inner work of the first six steps and the final steps, that emphasize my outer spiritual journey – changes in my walk with God. Will God really come into my life and lead me out?

In Isaiah 57:14-15-18, I learn "I will say, rebuild the past! Clear away the rocks and stones so my people can return from captivity'...I refresh the humble and give new courage to those with repentant hearts...'"

God is my ultimate help in clearing the

way to a better future. When I come to him with humility, admitting that I still struggle with many of my shortcomings, God refreshes me and gives me the courage I need to continue the battle.

Luke 18:10-14   Step 7

Considering my behavior, I sometimes feel unworthy to ask God for anything. My sins of my past still haunt me. I sometimes struggle with self-hatred. My remorse is genuine but I feel reluctant to approach God to ask for his help.

In Luke 18:10-14, I learn that God welcomes me even when I feel this way. Jesus tells this story. 'But the tax collector stood at a distance and dared not even lift his eyes to heaven as he prayed. Instead, he beat his chest in sorrow, saying, "O God, be merciful to me, for I am a sinner.' This sinner went home justified before God.

Tax collectors were among the most despised citizens in Jewish society. Jesus chose this illustration to emphasize that it doesn't matter where I fit in society's hierarchy. It is the humble heart that opens doors to God's love and forgiveness.

Philippians 2:5-9   Step 7

I no longer hide behind defenses during my spiritual recovery. I used to hide behind my good reputation, my important position, or a fantasy of my superiority...I have made a dramatic change in my attitude.

In Philippians 2:5-9, Paul wrote that Jesus is my ideal model for humility in obedience, love and service. My thoughts, attitudes and actions are to be patterned after him. His willingness to humbly obey His Father is a great example for me. As I look at my life honestly, I need to humbly admit my faults so I can begin to change my old patterns. Today, I have learned to admit my failures to him without hesitation.

I can ask God to change my attitudes. When God deals with my pride, I have stopped hiding behind my reputation.

I can allow myself to become anonymous knowing that I am another person struggling with my physical challenges and my addiction. When I humbly yield myself to God, he promises me future honor and restoration.

Leviticus 4:1-28   Step 8

I know when I allowed my life to get out of control. I probably hurt people without ever realizing it. In Leviticus 4:2, Paul writes that the meaning of the word sin is "to miss the mark." In the New Testament, the words of the apostle Paul tell me that I am a sinner and fall short of God's glorious standard. The Old and New Testament words for sin both emphasize the fact that it keeps me from experiencing the fullness of life that God wants me to enjoy. I know I have failed in some way, so God has provided a means for my healing and reconciliation. This means is available to me through repentance and obedience to God's plan for healthy living.

Ecclesiastes 4:9-12   Step 8

Loneliness and isolation go along with the guilt and shame I feel about who I am and what I've done. My deafness makes me feel cut off from others that I feel lonely even when I am around other people. My actions caused me guilt, fear of being hurt, and self-hatred. It is still hard for me to believe the love others have for me. By accepting their love, I am preparing myself to make amends.

King Solomon observed in Ecclesiastes 4:9-12, that supportive friends and healthy relationships are absolutely necessary for successful spiritual growth. When I fall down, I need help getting up again. As a profoundly deaf person, standing alone, I am especially vulnerable to inner enemies. I must learn to trust others, to reach out to others and to admit my need for others.

2 Corinthians 2:5-8   Step 8

A few of the things I've done have earned me disapproval and a loss of love. This fear of rejection has deterred me from reaching out to make amends.

In 2 Corinthians 2:5-8, Paul writes about a young man who was cut off from Church worship when his sins were made public. He turned around and tried to make amends, but some people refused to welcome him back into the Church.

There will be some people who respond with forgiveness, comfort, acceptance and love. This will help me overcome the grief, the bitterness and the discouragement I may feel.

Genesis 33:1-11   Step 9

Returning to someone I hurt is frightening. Over the years, a lack of communication, memories of anger and hateful emotional exchanges, create tremendous anxiety. There will be a time when I see that person face to face.

In Genesis 33:1-1, Esau seemed generously delighted to see his long lost brother. I can only speculate about his true feelings. This happy reunion certainly didn't signal the end of the brothers' feud. Conflict between their families continued throughout Old Testament times. The book of Obadiah records the joy that Esau's descendants, the Edomites', experienced over the Israelites defeat. Obadiah, an Israelite, joyfully announced the doom of Edom. In the New Testament, the hated family of Herod traced its lineage back to Esau. Conflicts are not easily resolved, but if they are left unresolved, they can become a burden to generations into the future.

Jacob's tremendous fear gave way to relief. The last time Jacob saw Esau, Jacob was in fear for his life. In time, both of them changed. Jacob faced his brother and found there was still affection, even though both remembered the pain.

Matthew 5:23-29   Step 9

I suffered brokenness in my life, in my relationship with God, and in my relationships with others. Brokenness weighed me down and can easily defeat me if I allow. My spiritual recovery isn't complete until all areas of brokenness are healed with my family, clergy, teachers, friends and bosses.

In Matthew 5:23-29, Jesus taught that I need to love God and also my Christian brothers and sisters. If I don't love people who I can see, how can I love God who I cannot see?

My spiritual walk involves repairing the brokenness in my life. I need to make peace with God, with myself and with others whom I alienated. Unresolved issues in my relationships may keep me from being at peace with God and myself. Step 9 is imperative in achieving this serenity.

1 Peter 2:18-25   Step 9

I have experienced major changes in my attitudes. I was so consumed by my physical challenges and alcoholism that I thought only of myself, failing to show any consideration for others.

The apostle Paul wrote in Philippians

2:3-4, don't be selfish; don't live to make a good impression on others, In 1 Peter 2:20-23, Peter wrote, "If you suffer for doing right and are patient beneath the blows, God is pleased with you…He never sinned, and he never deceived anyone…He left his care in the hands of God, who always judges fairly."

1 Timothy 4:7-8   Step 10

I'm amazed what I can achieve through consistent disciplined effort. Being a seasoned marathon runner, I realize that my rigorous training gives me a goal.

In 1 Timothy 4:7-8, Paul Writes, "Spend your energy in training yourself for spiritual fitness. Physical exercise has some value, but spiritual exercise is much more important."

Spiritual strength and agility come only through practice. I need to develop my spiritual muscles through consistent effort and daily discipline.

2 Timothy 2:1-8   Step 10

In my spiritual walk, I will some battles but lose others in the war to achieve wholeness. I get discouraged at times when I can't see any progress, even though I've been working hard. As I preserve through it all, I maintain the ground gained.

In 2 Timothy 2:3-7, Paul writes that

spiritual growth is never easy. My progress requires that I follow principles of disciplined faith on a daily basis. Like a soldier, I need to put aside the obstacles to my spiritual growth – my dependence, my chasing pleasures and my denial. As an athlete, I need to follow the rules for healthy living – God's will for my life.

If I stop working my spiritual program before reaching the goal, I may lose everything I have fought, trained and worked for.

Psalm 27: 1-6   Step 11

I turned to God initially to free me from the bondage of my physical challenges with deafness and alcoholism. Today, I am surprised to find that, as time passes, I turn to God because I desire to be near him.

In Psalm 27:1-6, David found great joy by improving his conscious contact with God. God is always there, but I am not always aware of his presence. My relationship with God usually begins with his meeting my desperate pleas. When I focused on getting to know God as an end, I discover he will give me what I always desired – the happiness of being close to my loving Father.

Psalm 105:1-9   Step 11

As I continue my spiritual walk, I need the strength to move along the path God wants me to follow. This strength comes as I visualize God's constant presence with me.

In Psalm 105:1-8, the psalmist writes that God always keeps his word. He fulfills all promises. God promised Abraham and Jacob that their descendants would inherit the land of Canaan. Generations after Jacob's death, the Israelites entered Canaan. God's promises take time to be fulfilled. I need to embrace God's spiritual promises for the long haul in life.

Isaiah 61:1-3 Step 12

My life being set free from my physical challenges with deafness and alcoholism by

God is a beautiful sight to see. As I practice these principles and share my experiences, people will see the glory of God in my life and gain hope. The path to love one's self is a life long voyage. I do not walk alone. I have the beauty of my twelve-step program and the book of Love –the Bible to carry me on this path.

May your path be blessed with the love of God and know you don't walk alone.

Author's Note

Bible verses were quoted from The Life Recovery Bible —New Living Translation

Tyndale House Publishers, Inc.
Wheaton, Illinois

Martin J. McNamara

Made in the USA
Charleston, SC
17 April 2013